A HISTORY OF
DEVON COUNTY COUNCIL
1889-1989

JEFFREY STANYER

The publication of this book to mark the
Centenary of the Devon County Council
has been financed by
Barclays Bank PLC.

DEVON BOOKS

First published in Great Britain in 1989 by Devon Books

ISBN: 0 86114–851–7

British Library Cataloguing-in-Publication Data
CIP Catalogue Record for this book is available from the British Library

Printed and bound in Great Britain by Vine & Gorfin Ltd

DEVON BOOKS

Official Publisher to Devon County Council
An imprint of Wheaton Publishers Ltd,
a member of Maxwell Pergamon Publishing Corporation plc

Wheaton Publishers Ltd
Hennock Road, Marsh Barton, Exeter, Devon EX2 8RP
Tel: 0392 74121; Telex 42794 (WHEATN G)

SALES

Direct sales enquiries to Devon Books at the address above

Contents

Bibliographical note

It is important for all readers, whether in higher education, local government itself or the community at large, to accept that underlying the account and analysis presented here are a number of academic concepts and theories that have been developed in spheres of wider scope than Devon County Council. A general framework of analysis is set out in J. Stanyer, *Understanding Local Government*, Fontana, 1976, reprinted by Martin Robertson, 1980; county government is explained in J. Stanyer, *County Government in England and Wales*, Library of Political Studies, Routledge & Kegan Paul, 1967, and chapter 9 of the 1976 volume. The concept of federalism is discussed in K. C. Wheare, *Federal Government*, Oxford University Press, first edition 1946, and refined in M. J. C. Vile, *The Structure of American Federalism*, Oxford University Press, 1961. The analysis of patterns of evolution within political organisations is derived from N. W. Polsby, 'The Institutionalisation of the House of Representatives', *American Political Science Review*, 62/1, 1968. The study of the processes of recruitment, socialisation and 'control' within organisations is based on A. Etzioni, *A Comparative Analysis of Complex Organisations*, The Free Press of Glencoe, 1961. The internal structure of organisations is analysed in terms of three 'systems' – operational, status and power – in T. Burns & J. M. Stalker, *The Management of Innovation*, Tavistock Publications, 1961, and the crucial relationship between individual needs and group demands is highlighted in C. Argyris, *Interpersonal Competence and Organisational Effectiveness*, Tavistock Publications, 1962. The theoretical perspective on participation in groups, organisations and associations is that of Mancur Olson, *The Logic of Collective Action*, Harvard University Press, 1965.

No further reference will be made to the sources of ideas.

The main sources of information relating to the County Council have been the Council's own minutes and reports and local newspapers, in particular the *Western Morning News*, the *Express and Echo*, the *Western Daily Mercury* and the *Western Times*. I have also consulted a considerable number of published studies but most do not contain much hard information of the sort that is needed for a centenary history. I am, however, grateful for the insights that they have provided into specific episodes, aspects of administration and personalities.

No individual references are given to the sources of information for each set of facts. Lack of space forbade this as a policy but in most cases the sources should be obvious to the reader.

PREFACE

This small volume commemorates the first hundred years of Devon County Council as a local authority in the English, and therefore United Kingdom, system of government. In so few words it is impossible to do justice to the richness, diversity and complexity of the County Council's development since the passage of the *Local Government Act, 1888*. Even the seven months from August, 1888, when individuals began to announce their candidatures, through January 24th, 1889, when the first councillors met as the provisional council, to April 1st, 1889, when it became the legal authority, exhibit on close examination a complicated story that can only be fully described by itself at greater length than is provided for the whole book. The last seven months of the century have been no less complex and confusing.

It is hoped to place copies of the 'raw material' gathered and systematised for this work in the County Library system for the benefit of future research and to enable those who have interests in specific subjects to look further into them.

The creation of county councils was accompanied by some 'doomsday' predictions of failure and the collapse of county administration and since that time they have had, as an institutional form, little theoretical support from the press and the academic world. But since 1889 public services have expanded several-fold and county councils have taken up more than a proportionate share of this growth. As the history of Devon County Council shows, this form of local government has become more important in the British political system with the passing of each decade. This volume attempts to portray the development of the County Council as an organisation playing an increasing role in public affairs and offers explanations of why the system evolved in the ways that it did, with minimum controversy, crisis and disruption.

In writing a centenary volume there are the opposed temptations and dangers: to give excessive attention to the very early years or to concentrate very largely on the current situation. I have deliberately tried to avoid the distortion that too much emphasis on either of these would give; in the eyes of the historian all years are equal and 'entitled' to their fair share of space. I have also tried not to favour one service over all the others. Undoubtedly, in terms of money spent and staff employed, some are more weighty than others; some also are much more in the public eye or are more likely to create public controversy. This is not, however, a history of separate public services but a study of an organisation which has experienced gains, losses and modifications of public functions and duties over a hundred years, but which is not so closely associated with any one of these as to depend on it for its identity.

I have been asked on many occasions whether Devon County Council will live to celebrate its second centenary. Though this is not strictly part of my present terms of reference I have indicated at various places the forces and factors which relate to answers to this question.

Thanks are due to Barclays Bank for providing the financial sponsorship which enabled the research to be continued and the book published, to the members and officers of the present County Council for their help, to numerous citizens of Devon who offered information, to the staff of the County Library and the County Record Office for assistance with research materials, to Brian Brady for the logistics of the project, to the staff of Devon Books for their understanding and co-operation, to the University of Exeter for providing me with support and facilities for research into 'county affairs' for nearly thirty years, to the Social Science Research Council for a small grant in 1967 and to Julia James for her work on the 'quantitative' aspects of County Council history.

The judgements made and opinions expressed in the book are the sole responsibility of the author for whom the writing of the book is in part the discharge of a moral obligation to those who have, over a long period of time, supported his research and provided him with ideas and evidence with which develop an understanding of the role of local government in political systems.

1

INTRODUCTION

A few words of introduction, perhaps even warning, are needed for all readers of this book. Many will notice that a considerable number of subjects which they expected to find in it have been omitted or are dealt with only very briefly. Part of the reason for this is that the maximum length of the book has meant that it has to be an essay and interpretation rather than a narrative and description of a very elaborate organisation with a long history. For instance, about 950 individuals have served on the County Council since 1889, an uncounted number have sought election but failed, and several hundred have been involved in county administration through co-option to committees. To do descriptive justice to these alone would take more than the whole book. Their characters and contributions have therefore been summarised and presented as broad generalisations.

The same point applies to chief officers. Though the County Council started with very few employees, over the decades the number and variety of professions that it employed increased more than tenfold. To do descriptive justice to these alone would take as much space as that devoted to council members. When the employees lower down the hierarchy – at headquarters, in the area and field offices, and in depots and institutions – are added, the need for interpretative generalisation is seen to have become acute.

The main task of the biographer of a local authority must be to try to identify the special character of the area studied, without inflating its significance to an indefensible degree. In the case of Devon it is not hard to discover that it has had a geographical and organisational identity of its own for many centuries but that the later decades of the twentieth century have tended to make it more like many other areas. The period embraced by this study – one hundred years – shows the County Council evolving very slowly and distinctively for perhaps eight decades though always having to respond in some way to events at national level, and then suddenly, over less than ten years, being transmuted into a very different social and political system.

The reader must not, however, expect a story that is completely new to a person with a general knowledge of English history. The student of an city or county finds him- or herself frequently concluding that the development of

1

the chosen local authority clearly reflects events at national level, and to a considerable extent shares its history with all, most or many of the others. The historical development of any individual local authority results from the formative influences of national and local factors. Devon, for instance, originally came into existence as part of the political system of Wessex and this grew into the Kingdom of England and into the United Kingdom of Great Britain and Ireland. During these centuries the County shared a common general history with other counties but also evolved in its own distinctive way, so that its 'biography' is a mixture of familiar and unfamiliar. All areas have special features and country-wide forces have different effects in different places because of these features. Thus, though Devon as an area was much less affected, on a millenial perspective, by the reforms of the 1960s and 1970s than were the conurbation counties and the shires of Eastern England, it had to accept the changes in the system of local government finance which the centre introduced one after another in the 1980s. A territory such as Devon, comprising only a small proportion of the total area and population of the state, cannot expect to be insulated or immune from the forces generated by the national economy, Westminster and Whitehall and, since the second world war, the international political and economic systems.

Devon County Council as a Local Authority

Fortunately, when the subject is an individual local authority, there are clear principles of selection and interpretation which can guide the writer in what are undoubtedly difficult and unwelcome decisions.

First, as a large organisation the County Council includes a great number of people whose work would be very much the same whether they were employed in an appointed local body, a field office or a private agency. Thus the testing of samples of food and drugs, the teaching of A-level French, the digging of a ditch, the putting-out of fires, the purchase of typing paper – all these involve technical activities which would happen if the employer was a quango, a government ministry or a multi-national corporation. It is this fact which makes much of the present Government's privatisation and 'contracting-out' policy feasible. The biographer must be aware of all these types of work – and many more – as part of the 'real' local authority, but they are part of the iceberg below the water. Only if the distinctive character of the organisation as a local authority affects them overtly should they be noticed. Thus, if there is pressure on inspectors to be lenient in their judgements, if a decision is taken to make all schools teach peace studies, if local firms are given a monopoly of stationery supplies, if the fire brigade has much better equipment than its neighbours, then the student of local government is rightly interested.

Secondly, all local authorities are governed, in England and Wales, by a body corporate consisting of elected individuals who, once elected, serve in their own right. The work of the council members provides a complex but clear pattern for decision-making because the electoral process divides up the years into groups which have an identity of their own and each year has to embody a definite sequence of actions. County councils have been required to hold their own 'general elections' at stated intervals – three-yearly from 1889–1970 and four-yearly from 1973 – and all directly elected members have come up for re-election at that time. Local elections were suspended during the two world wars so that those originally scheduled for 1916, 1940 and 1943 were cancelled.

	Ordinary Elections				
	1889–1918	1919–1945	1946–1972	1973–1989	total
number	9	7	9	4+1989	30

County councils took over from Quarter Sessions the cycle of quarterly meetings of the full authority and its committees and subcommittees. The cycle ran from year to year, starting with the annual meeting in spring, and including a budgetary procedure. The annual meeting formally laid down the pattern for the coming year but once the system had got over its 'teething troubles' there was a strong tendency to carry on the organisation from year to year with only the occasional incremental change.

The meeting cycle dominated the lives of all council members and all senior and middle-range officers. Only low-level clerical and manual workers were not directly affected by the inexorable succession of meetings. Work originated in meetings and had to be continued and completed by other meetings. Committees, for instance, had to meet at the right time to transact their share in the estimating of income and expenditure for the coming year, and professional officers had to make sure that draft estimates were ready.

For council members this still remains a major factor in their 'council lives'. Meeting succeeds meeting in an organised schedule and ordinary members calculate their 'workloads' in terms of the demands the committee system, in its widest sense, makes on them. But since the end of the Second World War several developments, described later, have reduced the dominance of the headquarters-standing-committee system.

Thirdly, the County Council was and is a multi-functional body, that is, it is responsible for a range of services rather than restricted to one or a very small number of related activities. The list of powers and duties has changed from time to time, mainly an expansion but occasionally a reduction of numbers. Increasingly over the years the County Council has come to fit into the overall system of state action as a 'doer', that is, as the actual provider of the services. It needs to employ competent scientific, technical and professional staff and there is pressure from several sources to make provision for 'state of the art' expertise. From the inclusion of many different professions within the Council's staff come many of the distinctive problems of internal organisation that are central to the interests of the student of local government.

Fourthly, the County Council has a highly organised environment. It is surrounded by other public bodies with whom it has to interact both formally and informally. The most important of these are the district councils within its boundaries who collectively administer the same territory, though mainly for different activities, deal with the same 'consumers', and derive from the same social and political system. The second most important are the 'branches' of public corporations, quangos and central ministries who are responsible for the services most closely related to the work of the County Council. The third group consists of private bodies with a county-wide area who are also responsible for activities that are closely related to those of the County Council.

Though county councils have become major service providing agencies in their own right they have also retained their role of overview and 'guardianship' of the county as a whole. The simple point is that if Devon County Council does not look after county affairs no-one will; certainly not the district councils, certainly not ad-hoc agencies such as health and water authorities, certainly not private bodies such as unions, churches and trade associations. But there is nothing in the law of the land which guarantees that a county council will take a county-wide view. It might be 'captured' by the representatives of an area or an economic or social interest.

The historian's interest, therefore, is in the relations between the County Council and its highly structured environment, in particular in explanations of why it was or was not 'taken over' by elements in its surroundings. Devon County Council has always involved itself very closely with a wide range of interests, territorial and sectional, through the organisation of its working processes. When substantive decisions have been under consideration it has never been a self-contained inward-looking authority. One of the most important changes in Devon during the hundred years has been the reform of its district structure. In 1889 lower level administration was in the hands of several different types of district and parish authority, none of whom were large enough to exert an individual influence on the County Council. A considerable rationalisation took place in 1894 but it left Devon with no lower tier authority comprising a noticeable part of the total. This situation remained until the 1970s when the abolition of all the small town and rural districts and the accession of the urban areas of Plymouth, Exeter and Torbay transformed the relations between county council and district councils. The number was reduced from 40 to 10, of which Plymouth contains a quarter of Devon's population, Exeter and Torbay together contribute nearly another quarter and even the smallest area – West Devon with 44,000 inhabitants – is large by pre-reorganisation standards.

The main regret must be in having to devote so little space to central-local relations and finance as separate topics. One of the reasons for not dealing with the former at more length comes from the fact that a major part of the subject lies in the centre and is shared with all other local authorities. The general national story has been told, with varying degrees of partiality, many times and it was not possible to do research on the perception of Devon County Council in Whitehall and Westminster. The same is also largely true of finance. This has become such a technical subject that it can only be described at great length. For Devon, however, the problem is in a sense relatively straightforward; the Government will make the changes it wants irrespective of the views of the County Council and the only actions that can be taken by the Authority as an individual are reactive. The realities of financial history can be seen through the changing role of the Council's chief financial officers and the decisive date is 1929, not 1979.

4

The Concept of the Local Authority as a Social System

Since the late 1950s local government studies have been revolutionised by the development and acceptance of research into one or a defined group of local authorities as local socio-economic and political systems in their own right – as individual areas and organisations. The theoretical perspectives that have been imported into the subject derive from modern political and economic history, sociology, social anthropology, geography, organisation studies and behavioural political science.

This study of Devon applies ideas derived from the above to the County Council as an individual social system and formal organisation. There is a tradition amongst academic analysts, particularly those of a reformist frame of mind, of regarding many of the problems of local government as arising from the short-sightedness of individual local authorities who have consistently pursued their own interests and acted on their own perceptions of reality: they have not sought the common good of all local authorities and the public interest in a strong local-government system.

This tradition is based on a misunderstanding of social rationality. Each local authority has interests which it shares with all, many, some or a few others; it also has divergent interests which may be much more weighty to it. It is not necessarily sensible for the individual social actor – such as a local authority – to pursue an interest in common with others regardless of the social, economic and political context in which it occurs. When the County Council's Association approached Devon County Council in 1890 it refused to join. This decision was reversed a year later and since that time it has sent its representatives to the Association. In the early years these were members who were also active in national politics. Because there is now a separation of county and national political leadership this can no longer occur, but the 'good standing' of Devon has recently been reflected in the election of one of its members to a leading position in the Association and the role of some of its chief officers as advisors in their spheres of expertise. But when the central government modifies the grant system, as it does now almost yearly, the changes are evaluated by the County Council in Devon terms, that is, by reference to their impact on its budget. It would be foolish to do otherwise.

Institutionalisation of political organisations

Research elsewhere has shown that over a period of time an elected body – an assembly, a legislature or a local council – may become institutionalised: that is, its boundaries become more clearly drawn, it is more difficult to enter and the differences between members and non-members more obvious; its internal complexity and sophistication increase, promoting the satisfaction of members and its effectiveness relative to the outside world; it moves towards automatic, universalistic criteria for making organisational decisions. The reversal of this process, which usually results from a changing environment, is de-institutionalisation whose signs are disputes involving personalities, lack of courtesy, legal writs, paranoia, abuse and personal criticism, the involvement of officials, disputes over organisational matters (standing orders,

5

points of order, 'promotions', 'patronage'), low attendance and high turnover rates and low commitment to the organisation.

Devon County Council exhibited a classic pattern of development, with only short episodes of disruption, which fits the model of institutionalisation very closely. The process can also be called 'modernisation' because, although there were forces in Devon which opposed the general trends in society, eventually the County Council came to adopt procedures, methods and policies which were becoming the general practice in other parts of the country.

At both council-member and officer levels the County Council became more systematically and rigorously organised. Roles became clearer and the rules by which decisions about individuals were made became 'conventions of the local constitution'. These changes are symbolised by the gathering together of headquarters staff, who had previously been scattered on an *ad hoc* basis throughout central Exeter, in a purpose-built County Hall. In real terms, however, the systematic organisation of relations between County Council and county district councils, which has become a feature of the post-1973 system, was more significant. The institutionalisation extended to relations with other public bodies within its proximate environment, particularly the machinery of justice, the National Health Service and the administration of the water cycle. The growing importance of the management of 'boundary' relations is symbolised by changes in the County Council's Yearbook, which now presents the authority's interactions with other agencies as a major part of its organisation.

Work, status and power

All formal organisations embody three distinct 'structures': an operating system, a status system and a power structure. In the long run the three are likely to be congruent, but for short periods they may not coincide and this generates tension and disruption. Relations between 'work' activities, social prestige and the ability to 'make things happen' constitute one of the main forces moulding the evolution of the organisation and creating the 'goods' and 'bads' experienced by individuals as a result of membership.

For the first half of the century status within Devon County Council reflected status in a sharply differentiated world outside it. But this was of declining importance decade by decade until it was largely replaced by *party* as an external source of power. Belonging to a political organisation that could command votes and win seats became more significant than enjoying social prestige in county society. But the decision-making system required individuals who would work hard at the leading operational roles and any one who was able and willing to do this was able to acquire status and influence within the system. During every decade individual council members created a position for themselves on the County Council by contributing to the working of the decision-making system. Operational importance created status and power within the social and political systems of the local authority.

Similar developments took place in the official sector. In the early years the socially long-established professions of law, accountancy, architecture, civil engineering and medicine were operationally the most important and as far as one can judge enjoyed a commensurate status. In the twentieth century the County Council added the semi-professions of education, social work and 'cultural' administration. New spheres of technical activity such as town and country planning had to make their way within an engineering framework, and management services began under the general frameworks of law and finance. By the 1960s there were so many 'chief' officers that the Council had to start distinguishing between them in terms of membership of the leadership group. This has been formalised by the creation of a management team with designated members.

Power is hard to detect and measure but it is to be presumed that factors similar to those influencing elected representatives exist at official level. The length of service of the individual, the size of department he or she heads and the way it fits into the overall decision-making structure are obvious sources of power within the official sector of the local authority.

The concept of the 'three systems' connects the processes of institutionalisation and de-institutionalisation above with the inevitable tension all organisations experience between their systemic demands and the needs of their individual members.

Tension between individual needs and systemic demands

Both the individual and the organisation are living organisms and there is a tension and conflict between their respective demands and needs. Thus if certain things do not happen, for instance if certain roles are not filled or are acted out in different ways, the organisation may experience 'decay' and will be judged to have 'failed'. But unless the system also offers leaders and lower participants sufficient personal rewards and satisfactions to offset the personal costs of belonging it will find that members do not make the needed contributions and leave the organisation at the earliest opportunity.

Service on Devon County Council was costly to the individual and only those who could personally afford the time and money involved in membership offered themselves for election and remained on the Council. The system, therefore, had to provide 'rewards' to offset these costs. It seems obvious, though it cannot be proved, that for those who were not originally of high social status in the local community, service on the County Council had the effect of raising their visibility and providing a basis for recruitment to other public and private bodies. The highest level of individual reward was inclusion in the Honours List which was achieved by several Council chairmen.

In the postwar years payment of expenses and compensation for loss of earnings was introduced and has become more elaborate over time until it provides a system which goes some way to offsetting the personal costs of council membership. But no-one would seek election solely for the monetary rewards and the system must be regarded as facilitating rather than motivating. Willingness to serve must therefore be accounted for by more intangible factors – in the relations between the County Council and local society and in 'life' within the organisation itself.

Recruitment, socialisation and 'control'

All organisations require a continuing flow of new members to replace those who die or resign, and these 'newcomers' need to be introduced to the culture and working activities of the system so that at least some of them become valued participants whose contribution helps to maintain its effectiveness. For local authorities this is an acute matter. Leaders have only influence over 'backbenchers', not formal control, and this is modified by the reciprocal powers of every council member as a legally equal participant in the system. The lack of formal power of control at council and committee meetings throws all the responsibility on to the processes of recruitment and socialisation. The types of people found in an organisation are influenced by the 'incentives' it can offer and further modified by the ongoing processes that operate continuously. Recruitment and socialisation thus help to integrate the individual and the organisation and reduce the tension and conflict between the two.

In the case of Devon the factor of pre-socialisation was of considerable importance. New members tended to come from environments in which the County Council was well-known and understood and from other public bodies in which many of the same basic processes operated. Once on the Council the newcomer found him- (and lately her-) self in a minority surrounded by long serving members who provided models of behaviour. In such circumstances the culture of the organisation is easily passed from cohort to cohort. The system also provided a wide range of activities amongst which any individual could find a selection which was personally satisfying. Even when this was not true in the first instance the committee system provided a series of miniature environments in which values and interests were acquired as a result of service within them.

2

THE CENTENARY OF COUNTY COUNCILS

U ntil the 1960s counties were distinctive features of the maps of all parts of the United Kingdom and the Republic of Ireland. Traditional atlases always contained a coloured map showing the ancient counties and school children learned their names and the name of their county town. They were the basis for the territorial organisation of many social, economic and political activities and many people were aware and proud of the county of their birth.

It was, however, as units of government that they were most important. Other functions often derived from the fact that they were levels of both central and local government. For many centuries they were the only large-scale geographical element in the political systems of the British Isles. They served as areas of field administration for the centre and as major areas for local self-government – though not local democracy – until the end of the nineteenth century. In the twentieth century the national government has developed alternative patterns of local areas and a regional dimension for some services but it still uses the county as a basis for organisation for many of its activities. In the twentieth century, also, the county developed as a complex form of local democracy which often baffles academics and participants alike.

Since the beginning of the 1960s, however, some inroads have been made into the universality of the county in the British Isles. The first departures were in the mid–1960s with the merger of small counties in the east Midlands and the creation of Greater London. Both of these can be regarded as responses to changing circumstances, the first as the elimination of weak areas and the second as an adaption of the principles to the circumstances of a metropolis and capital city. In the 1970s, some new counties were created in England, though many of the ancient ones remain visible on the map. The territorial maps of Wales, Scotland and Northern Ireland, however, were completely redrawn, so that, paradoxically, only Southern Ireland, on whom counties were imposed by alien rulers, retains the traditional territorial pattern. There have also been radical proposals for reform – mainly by outsiders – which would have obliterated all long-established boundaries and removed virtually all signs of Saxon and Norman government from the administrative landscape of England.

The county and the county council, however, are not identical. Counties as areas can exist with or without a county council. The latter were created as recently as 1888–89 and it is this fact which is being marked in England and Wales in 1989.

The two years 1988 and 1989 contain a series of centenaries that derive from the *Local Government Act, 1888*, often referred to as 'the County Councils Act'. In 1988 March 19th was the anniversary of the introduction of the Bill that eventually became the Act; the legislative process ran from that date to the Royal Assent on August 13th. The autumn saw the drawing up of the Register of Electors which came into operation on January 1st, 1889, and the creation, by the Local Government Board, of a system of electoral divisions for each county. In 1989 each county council had the anniversaries of its first elections – between January 14th and 31st – and of the first meeting of the provisional council – on the second Thursday after the election. Finally, April 1st marks the end of provisional status and the start of a hundred years of county council meetings; the provisional council became fully operational at a meeting on that day.

It is well known that the reforms introduced in these two years had been a very long time – over fifty years – in the making and that they were unfinished, that is, everyone expected them to be completed in the near future. The legislation of 1888 was rounded out by further statutes enacted in 1894 and 1899. It is less well appreciated that the process had to be repeated for Scotland (1889) and Ireland (1898) so that by 1900 there existed in all parts of the United Kingdom two distinctive types of local government which, in the language of analysis, are *simple* and *complex* systems. 1988 and 1989 are also anniversaries of county boroughs, but as these did not survive beyond 1974 there is no pressure to mark the relevant dates. It is also the case that the status of 'county borough' had clear and exact precedents in the 'cities of counties' and 'counties corporate' of the unreformed system.

County Government in the British Isles

The word 'county' has a number of different meanings within the govern-mental systems of the British Isles. Sometimes it refers to the 'ancient' or 'geographical' counties, many of which date back to Saxon times, whose administrative, but not social and cultural, significance has disappeared. On other occasions it refers to the local government areas which were administra-tive counties from 1888 to 1974 and metropolitan and non-metropolitan counties since 1973. In particular contexts it denotes quarter sessions which had responsibility for the whole county area before 1889 and the county council which took over this role in that year.

In respect of the first two meanings Devon now has boundaries which make the governmental county coincide overwhelmingly with the ancient county. But the County Council is not the only local authority within the area of Devon and its role must be understood in the light of its relations with other councils having jurisdiction within its territorial limits. It is a mistake to equate the County Council with the County.

When a major reform – or a revolution – takes place there is always considerable interest in the question 'how innovatory are the changes?'. Usually at the time there are both optimists and pessimists – millenarians and doomsters, 'white' and 'black' utopians – who disagree about the desirability of the reform and make opposed predictions about the future.

County government was intended to provide for the administration of those tracts of the state's territory which consisted of medium and small towns, villages and the countryside. County government was not and is not simply rural local government, but large towns and great cities everywhere have always had both the capacity and the will to govern themselves, and usually also the power to obtain a status of autonomy relative to the areas surrounding them. The big mediaeval towns escaped from the direct control of royal agents and the smaller ones gained a lesser degree of freedom from the administration of the surrounding hundred. In modern geographical language they were central places and in traditional language they were a special sort of liberty – the borough.

Counties as complex systems of local government

Counties in the British Isles are complex systems of local government in which what happens is only intelligible if it is interpreted in a context which includes two or more levels of government and politics. County councils were originally intended to be intermediate bodies, taking some of the load of central control from Whitehall and Westminster, rather than major service providers. Since Edwardian times, however, the upper tier has grown at the expense of the lower, and especially after the reorganisation of public services in the late 1940s, the county council's role has been transformed and its position as the leading element in county government has been strengthened.

The study of an individual county council must take into account the fact that it was always the main element in the system and thus the object of the attentions of both 'higher' and 'lower' public authorities. It finds itself harassed from below by its districts and from above by the central government. Every demand made from either of these sources is a potential threat to the stability of the system; though most do not do more than ruffle the surface others are in prospect more serious. The main problem is to explain how such bodies develop a *persona*, a style of government, which enables them to balance central demands – for efficiency and equality in service provision – with the values implicit in localism, some of which are definitely hostile to the whole ideology of the centre, and to avoid the system being thrown into some sort of disequilibrium.

There are many factors which contribute to the orderliness and stability of English local authorities and here only one of them is explored in detail. The 'harmony' of the system rested on the actions and activities of members of the County Council. This is not to assert that the members collectively decided matters or dominated other political and administrative institutions, nor that they exerted day-to-day control; their behaviour rather created a style and

11

tone of government which had far-reaching consequences for other parts of the local political system and for other political actors. What they did *not* do was as important as their positive actions.

The county council as a local authority

The study of an individual county council must therefore take into account a number of factors. First, there is the question how far the existence of different levels of local government within a county corresponds to or reflects the existence of different levels in county society; in particular, how far there is a county identity distinct from local town and village allegiances. Secondly, the existence of districts and parishes impinges implicitly and explicitly on substantive decision-making by the county council and on the provision of services; as a local authority a county council has always to be aware of the other councils within its boundaries.

A third major factor arises from the the centrally inspired process of re-allocation of services between levels, sometimes downwards but usually upwards during this period, and the removal or redefinition of governmental functions to decrease or increase substantive roles for councils. County councils gained services at the expense of districts in the 1940s and lost powers to regional 'quangos' in the 1970s. On balance, however, county councils have their present character as authorities because they were the net gainers from the processes of redistribution of public functions.

County councils as intermediate authorities

County councils inherited from Quarter Sessions a tutelage function. The county level of government had always carried out supervisory roles; it was intermediate between the national government in London and the lowest levels of local administration in villages, small and medium-sized towns in the sense that it carried out the state function of integrating small areas – localities – in the national governmental system within its own defined boundaries. When writers talk about local administration before the nineteenth century they often intend to refer to territorial jurisdictions smaller than a county. There is evidence that national political leaders hoped that the county councils would relieve some of the burdens of central control that had become noticeable since the 1830s with the introduction of 'national' services, minimum standards of efficiency and effectiveness, and central grants to local authorities. Before the County Council had ceased to be provisional there was talk in Devon of additional central government roles being delegated to it.

Thus in the 1890s the county council had major supervisory roles in respect of the organisation [status, boundaries and elections] of districts and parishes within its boundaries and in the framing of by-laws; it had default powers in respect of a number of lower level services; it could increase the amount of indirect administration by delegating duties to other bodies; it was responsible for equity and equalisation in the system of local taxation; it contributed to other public agencies through the right of appointment or nomination to membership. These powers played a part from time to time in Devon local government – the 1930s saw the county review of district and parish boundaries, every third year problems arose with the electoral process in a minute number of parishes, and awkwardness arose through having to report a district to the Local Government Board for failing to provide an adequate sewerage system. In addition, the County Council had to offer general assistance when it was necessary, for instance, in the case of natural disasters, or where a function involved economies of scale that a small authority could not exploit.

One implication of this was that county authorities, whether appointed quarter sessions or elected councils, did not need very large permanent fulltime paid staffs. The bureaucratic or directly employed element in county administration was relatively small and this meant that the 'lay' members had to fill executive roles that would normally have been carried out by paid officials. Many of the substantive functions of local government were actually provided by other public bodies – some local authorities, some part of the machinery of justice and others local 'quangos' – and by public officials appointed by the county council but having a degree of autonomy in the exercise of their powers. The tutelage role has never disappeared completely but it has been swamped by the growth of county council responsibilities which were and are discharged through its own committees and officers.

Supervisory roles over, and the provision of services through, other bodies are essentially sensitive and discretionary; they require non-routine political skills and place an extra burden on elected members. The duties are particularly demanding because the intermediate authority is subject to conflicting pressures: from the centre for system-wide rationality, uniformity, and efficiency; from the localities for inconsistent special treatment, for 'bespoke' action, for exemptions – in effect for favouritism.

County councils as large authorities

A second important element in traditional county government was the provision of services and the carrying out of activities which were collective in the modern sense of that word and which transcended the interests and needs of small areas. In the case of bridges, for instance, a particular structure might connect only the fields of a single farmer, or two hamlets, or a village to the rest of the locality, or two distant towns, or one end of the kingdom with another. The effect of the industrial revolution was to increase geographical mobility – of labour, capital, goods and services, and private individuals – throughout the length and breadth of the land and this in its turn greatly broadened the area or geographical spread of 'gainers' (and 'losers') from any specific collective event, institution or condition. In modern language the extent of spillovers and externalities had greatly increased.

This role was also carried over to the post–1888 system. The identification of activities that had an impact beyond a very narrow local sphere remained a feature of county government until the process of transferring local government services from district to county council level was more or less over. Once the upper tier had become the major service provider such arguments as what was or was not a main road became of little practical importance. Political conflict shifted to questions of how far an area was getting its share of public goods in the form of county council services.

Not all counties were actually large in area and number of inhabitants – a fact which caused difficulties for the local government system in national politics – but Devon has never been a problem in this respect; in 1891 it was the second largest in terms of area and only 10 had larger populations. With the re-incorporation of the county boroughs in 1974 it has continued to be a large authority presiding over a wide range of environments. The present role which illustrates this point most clearly is that of promoting economic development.

Before County Councils

The first national 'event' – which starts the century – to affect the County of Devon was the reform of local government in 1888. By the 1880s virtually every type of local government authority in England and Wales, except the county, had acquired a reformed constitution in which the members of the governing body were elected by local people for a fixed, though renewable, term of office. But the largest areas, outside the counties corporate or 'cities of counties', remained untouched by the representative principle. Once boroughs had been modernised, and the hundred replaced by the union, county-level administration was an obvious anomaly in the pattern.

Before 1889 county government had been in the hands of the justices of the peace sitting in quarter sessions. Over the centuries a distinction had grown up between the judicial and administrative functions of the court and when it carried out the latter quarter sessions looked very much like a conventional local authority with its officials, committee system and financial procedures. By the 1880s it was a primary local authority except that the members of the authority were appointed, not elected. But though the justices were in formal terms centrally appointed they were also local people in the sense that the active ones were resident in the area and were often heavily involved in other spheres of public affairs.

Much of the work of quarter sessions in earlier centuries had been supervisory in the sense that it looked after authorities within its boundaries with smaller jurisdictions, acting in modern terminology as a tutelage authority rather than a direct service provider. During the nineteenth century it gradually acquired functions which forced it to develop its own internal organisation to provide services on a county-wide basis. In the case of Devon the process of administrative reform progressed very slowly because national law prevented the authority from delegating powers to committees and officers. Modernising the financial system proved particularly difficult and some of the problems carried over into the reformed structure.

But the administrative work of Quarter Sessions in Devon attracted the interest of and generated commitment from a number of leading Devon citizens – landowners, professionals and businessmen. In the eyes of the justices the executive work of the court was more significant than the judicial and when the former was completed many did not stay in Exeter for the latter. Everyone recognised that Quarter Sessions was within its limitations a reasonable working authority but it increasingly lacked legitimacy. The principle of direct election of local authorities had spread widely in the nineteenth century and 'no taxation without representation' served as a justified slogan with which to attack the oligarchic nature of county government.

The reform of county government

The first proposals for the reform of county government were put before Parliament in the 1830s and from 1836 to 1852 there was a series of unsuccessful attempts to create county boards to replace the justices as the administrative authority at county level. After 1852 the pressure seems to have abated a little but there was wide recognition that changes were necessary, and a number of inquiries were held.

The difficulties faced by reformers were several. First, there was no agreement about the form the new authority should take, because some supporters of change wished to retain an appointed element in the membership selection process. Secondly, the changes were evaluated by the representatives of some economic and social interests largely in terms of their financial effects, that is, their consequences for the rate-levying and expenditure processes. Both the agricultural and business interests had distinctive and opposed views of the 'fair' distribution of the burdens of local taxation. What would now be called 'management' reasons were, for these protagonists, sacrificed to considerations of political economy.

Thirdly, changes in organisational structure were often associated with proposals to reform or increase public services and activities. Leaders of interest sectors can easily work out the impact of new public functions on their 'constituencies' and the modernisation of county government was retarded by fears of what the new authorities would do. The democratisation of county administration in the nineteenth century might perhaps have occurred at an earlier stage if it had not been tangled up with other substantive issues such as the distribution of local financial burdens and the licensing laws. The conjunction of organisational and substantive issues, however, was probably inevitable because county-level authorities had always been the supervisor of smaller areas within their territorial jurisdiction and were expected to take an even greater role as intermediaries between central and local government, removing the 'burden' of control from Whitehall and Westminster to what was, in the social geography of the time, a regional level of government.

Fourthly, within each county the upper level or county-wide authority often had different relations with each of the boroughs within its boundaries. Some - the counties corporate or cities of counties – had escaped from the jurisdiction of quarter sessions centuries before, others enjoyed some but not all of the possible 'liberties' of a borough and a third category were outside the jurisdiction of the hundred authorities. But no simple classification was possible and the uncertainties of relative powers were frequently the subject of local political, financial and legal dispute.

In fact it was by no means clear what was a county in the nineteenth century. Some of the ancient counties had major subdivisions which sometimes acted as though they were separate areas with their own authority. This was a question which occupied the attention of Parliament at some length.

A final factor was constituted by the related questions of county boundaries and the structure of lower-tier local government within each county area. If county government was to be reformed it was highly desirable to draw the boundaries of county areas so that overlapping and other forms of incoherence between counties were eliminated and to remove the chaos of areas which constituted district level administration. But each type of lower level organisation, even the parish and the hundred, had its supporters, and eventually one had to be chosen as the basis of the new system and the others disbanded.

Few could deny that in the political atmosphere of the time county administration lacked legitimacy but two arguments were used to counter the reformers. First, it was argued that the county magistrates were in general effective administrators and elected councillors would do no better. Secondly, the fear was expressed that the representative principle actually would not work at the county level. The leaders of county society would not seek election to the new bodies and there were no viable alternative sources of political leadership. A new system, it was predicted, would literally collapse because no-one would be found to serve.

The recruitment of members, therefore, was identified as a major factor in the success or failure of reform. From the vantage point of 1989 it is known that the predictions of the pessimists and 'doomsday' prophets were in both the short and long runs unfulfilled. County councils almost immediately established themselves as viable and vital elements in the local government system and grew in importance relative to other local authorities in every decade after 1889. Of the English county areas existing today, fifteen have a shape almost identical with that of 1889, twelve are clearly 'rumps' of the original areas, and six are mergers of two or more. The remaining thirteen are to varying extents entirely new creations. The fact that they have attracted the support of 'the political classes' of successive generations is the key to understanding the absence of the instability predicted by the pessimists.

The 1888 Act

By the 1880s the reform of county government had become a bi-partisan matter. Though Liberals and Conservatives had differing views on many detailed issues there was wide acceptance of the general need for reform. The defection of the Liberal Unionists to Lord Salisbury pushed the latter's government decisively towards change and the measure introduced reflected previous Liberal efforts as well as Conservative thinking on the subject.

The Bill introduced on March 19th, 1888, which applied only to England and Wales, was a comprehensive measure for the reform of all levels of county government. It provoked extensive discussion and took up a very large amount of Parliamentary time but it was not the principle of election which was the main cause of trouble. Obviously there were some who thought that the justices should be retained or should be an added element to the new authority; others favoured indirect election; and there were several different proposals relating to the electoral system and method of voting. But it was always likely that the standard municipal constitution would be adopted in outline and this eventually occurred.

The main exception was in respect of the police. The supporters of retaining an appointed element were successful in creating a joint board as the police authority in each county. Each standing joint committee was to be composed of equal numbers of members nominated by the county council and by quarter sessions. This produced a contrast between the organisation of county and borough police forces which lasted until the 1970s.

In respect of financial change the Bill perhaps gained a degree of acceptability with some sectors because it reformed and extended the system of central grants to local authorities. It therefore promised some reduction of the 'burden' of local taxation. It did, however, leave the financial settlements between the new counties and the new 'county boroughs' to worked out on a local basis. In the case of Devon the negotiations dragged on for several years. It also proved necessary to redraw the division of local taxation between agriculture and the rest of the tax base in less than ten years.

The Bill was seen as an opportunity to reform the content and administration of certain public services and activities. The most important of these was licensing law. This provoked opposition from the temperance movement which saw the proposal as an attempt to create property rights in the sale of alcohol. The substance of the change was irrelevant to county government but it affected the acceptability of the whole package included in the Bill. It had to be dropped before the Bill became law.

The third problem was however central to county government reform. What was to happen to the boroughs that had not within living memory and generally much longer between within the jurisdiction of quarter sessions? The obvious answer was to give them the status of county in their right, but some of them were small, the degree of autonomy highly variable, and other urban areas not enjoying this historic position were much larger. As being a county-borough was likely to prove highly advantageous to an urban area the sources of confusion and uncertainty created the opportunity for deep political conflict over the achievement of this privileged position.

Finally, though the Government would have like to have reformed the structure of lower tier local government in a comprehensive measure, it was forced to drop the district council sections from the Bill and to straighten historic boundaries through a division of overlapping lower tier areas on very crude principles. Devon was not greatly affected by this, nor by the question what was a distinct county which caused considerable conflict in eastern England, Yorkshire, Hampshire and Sussex.

The general conception of multi-tier government was not, therefore, new to the British state. What was an innovation was the reorganisation of the whole structure, on a county by county basis, so that each county area had a coherent local government system within its own boundaries. The process by which this 'systematisation' was achieved is in modern language modernisation through 'democratisation' and 'managerial rationalisation'.

First, it created a council for the whole area with a uniform constitution copied from municipal government – from the franchise through to the internal organisation of committees and departments. The introduction of the county electoral register, the provision for direct election of the majority of members, the institution of the aldermanic bench for the remainder, the vesting of authority in a body corporate, the imposition of specific procedural requirements – these all contributed to the removal from the British administrative landscape of a long-standing problem – the unreformed oligarchic element in local government.

Secondly, it envisaged a coherent set of boundaries and areas; as a start all instances of overlapping and outliers were to be eliminated and the pattern of lower tier authorities reorganised and this was to be followed over a longer period by the adaptation of the structure to changing social geography. As events turned out the first process was carried out in a very crude manner, the second was delayed for six years, and the third evolved in a manner not predicted by the promoters of the Act.

Thirdly, it attempted to rationalise the system of local government finance by constructing a system of central grants that reflected the demands on local public expenditure. The county council had two roles; it was in charge of the general management of the local tax base and it was the main recipient of central grants.

The Act only applied to England and Wales but its relevance to Scotland and Ireland was immediately appreciated. Before the end of the nineteenth century the reform had been 'copied' for the rest of the United Kingdom and, until local government in Northern Ireland (1972) and Scotland (1975) was changed out of all recognition in the early 1970s, county government dominated the local government systems of the British Isles.

The comparative significance of the 1888 Act

The previous section includes a historical comparison with the traditional system of county administration in the British Isles. But there are other comparisons that can be made. During the fifty years of debate on the reform of the county some of the participants showed that they were aware of alternative forms of local government.

Outside the Anglo-Saxon world, local government is generally organised in principle as a hierarchic system, with the geographically smaller types being subordinates of the next level up the scale. The principle of hierarchy applies to both the councils as collective authorities and the employees as public servants. Two versions of this system exist in the modern world; the Napoleonic prefectoral state and the socialist state. What was created by the 1888 Act, and modified by a consistent pattern of evolution, was something that was above all non-hierarchical. It was not, however, a pattern that could easily be implemented outside the old dominions; British imperial and colonial administration closely resembled the prefectoral systems of western Europe.

In the United Kingdom reforms have never been whole-heartedly comprehensive and rigorous but a degree of systematic structuring has been achieved from time to time, to be followed by a dis-structuring over several decades which end with a partial re-structuring. During all these cycles, however, the idea of the county as a territorial unit has remained unchanged. The best introduction to the concept of county government is through the theory of federalism. Because most students of local government in Britain were familiar with the medium-sized or large city which had county-borough status every local authority tended to be treated as though it were a miniature unitary state, irrespective of whether it was part of a complex system or not. But those who have studied federalism (as opposed to the government of individual states) – America, Australia, Canada, Switzerland etc. – have focused on the problems of describing and analysing the overall structure of government and have quickly come to realise that a federal system is not just a unitary state with a big regional level of government added. The federal system is founded on both levels equally and simultaneously. Birch characterises federalism as co-operative, and undoubtedly co-operation plays a part in the working of such systems. But it is only a facet of the interdependence that Vile sees as the main structural characteristic of American federalism. Both levels have an existence independently of the other, both need complementary and supplementary actions by the other and each is able to exert influence on the other.

The 1888 Act created a system of local government in each county in which the distinct levels had their own authorities whose members were independently chosen and whose continued existence did not depend entirely or even largely on the goodwill of other bodies within the area. Some processes of decision-making legally required action by more than one authority whilst others through political necessity involved two or more levels in practice. The forms of political behaviour familiar to the student of federalism are to be found in county government. A distinction must therefore be drawn between the whole complex system of county government and the individual local authorities as specific elements of state organisation. This distinction has perhaps caused more difficulties and misunderstanding than most others within the study of local government. The county council, or upper tier authority, is part of a list which includes parishes, districts and local 'quangos', that is, other local authorities having a role within the boundaries of the county itself.

Temporal Change

One of the main themes of any history must be the relative contributions of different types of temporal change and the degree of continuity and stability that a system shows. History involves long-term trends, cycles and oscillations, discrete transitions from one stage to another – sometimes catastrophic – and random variations that are unique to the system. The basic problem is to distinguish long term trends from the stages of a cyclical process; for instance, does a flare-up in council member relations fore-shadow a move towards institutional decay or is it part of a cycle of excitement and quiescence? How far do random variations obscure more significant temporal changes or give the appearance of a quite different reality?

In the case of Devon County Council its history will be presented as a story of a very gradual evolution over a long period of time, brought to an end by the sharp discontinuity of reorganisation in 1971–74, and followed by a period of more rapid change and the search for a new pattern of stability.

The long-term trend was *modernisation*. Gradually over a long period, despite specific problems and opposition from 'backwoodsmen' the County Council evolved into a modern local authority and came to terms with the forces that were moulding all local authorities from the late nineteenth century onwards.

The history of the traditional County Council divides into three main periods: 1889–1918; 1919–1945; 1946–1973. The two world wars were the dividing episodes and could be linked with either the period before or the period after. In both cases, however, the judgement has been made that the war years look back more to the times before than forward to the times after. At the end of each war there was a sense of the necessity for a new start in society as a whole, epitomised by the slogan 'homes fit for heroes' in 1918 and the election of the Attlee government in 1945.

Within each major period there were significant events which contributed to the development of the system and perhaps marked minor periods in county history. The 1902 Education Act was a dividing point in the first period, and the 1929 Act clearly divided the 1930s from the 1920s. After 1945 the pace of social change in the County speeded up, so that the late 1940s constituted a time of uncertainty and rapid development, the 1950s wrongly gave the illusion of an era of relatively stability and the 1960s saw the start of the events that ended in 1974.

The post-reorganisation period has been marked by an accelerating pace of change originating ultimately in the international economic and political systems but passing through and modified by central government. From the point of view of the historian early 1989 is not a good date at which to pass judgement on the modern Devon County Council. Imminent and crucial elections will determine what sort of political system is to be embodied in the council and committee meetings, whilst the next five years will show how the changes in local government finance and service organisation will affect the County Council as a local authority.

3

DEVON AS A COUNTY

Devon has existed as a county, that is, as a major unit of English government, since the eighth century and has probably had its present shape, with only small variations, since the tenth century. In 1989, therefore, it is not the county as a traditional area that celebrates a first hundred years but its first form of popular government. Devon County Council came into full legal existence on April 1st, 1889, after ten weeks of provisional status. It was created as a consequence of the *Local Government Act, 1888* which provided for the discharge throughout England and Wales of the administrative functions of the centrally appointed justices acting in quarter sessions by an locally elected council.

The County of Devon

The ancient county of Devon had few external boundary problems. The early Ordnance Surveys and Parliamentary investigations in the 1820s revealed a few detached parts and anomalies beyond the Tamar and an exclave in Dorset, whilst there were two enclaves of the latter in east Devon, and some disputed areas on Exmoor. Compared with the main area of the County these were negligible in acreage and population, though this did not prevent them causing occasional conflicts with the neighbouring counties. The registration county – an aggregation of registration districts created by the centre in the 1830s – departed slightly from the geographical county but not to any substantial extent.

The main boundary problems were internal. The investigation of municipal corporations in the mid–1830s revealed that though most of the boroughs were too small to be a threat to Devon Exeter had been a county in its own right since the sixteenth century. There were also the urban growth points of Plymouth and Devonport which were creating a small conurbation in the south west corner. The relations between the County and its major urban areas were established as a theme in the nineteenth century and continue to exercise an influence today.

The rest of Devon, however, with its pattern of market towns was good terrain for the work of the assistant commissioners creating the new pattern of poor law areas in the mid–1830s. The map of union boundaries shows a regular system of areas which was the basis of lower tier organisation in 1872 (urban and rural sanitary districts) and in 1894 (non-county boroughs, urban districts and rural districts) – in fact, until 1974. The system was modified unsystematically by the use of local optional powers, particularly by coastal towns, to create improvement commissions, local boards, highway districts and other *ad hoc* authorities, so that by 1889 the County contained within its boundaries a 'chaos' of areas, authorities and rates. The hundred still existed on paper but had no local governmental function.

At the lowest level in the system parish government had been decaying for many decades. One of the problems was the unsatisfactory character of many parish boundaries. Many of the obvious problems were dissolved in the 1880s when Devon made considerable use of the powers of the Divided Parishes Acts to get rid of about 120 detached parts or anomalies through merger with the surrounding area. This provided the basis for the institution of modern parish government in 1894. From 1888 to 1934 there were about 40 changes in parish boundaries and in 1935 the Devon County Review Order made another 32. After the Second World War most of the changes were the result of boundary extensions by the county boroughs but a systematic review under the Local Government Boundary Commission for England began in the late 1970s. In recent years the County Council has taken an interest in parish government and has provided a headquarters for the parishes' own joint organisation.

From 1870 to 1902 one of the most important organisations at the parish level was the school board or school attendance committee for elementary education. The work of the boards in providing elementary education and the committees in enforcing attendance at church and chapel schools, however, was taken over by the County Council in 1902.

The internal structure of Devon immediately after the creation of the County Council [based on the 1891 census] was as follows:

3 county boroughs	17 poor law unions,
9 municipal boroughs	22 urban sanitary districts
33 hundreds	16 rural sanitary districts
451 civil parishes	

The municipal boroughs were also urban sanitary districts, making a total of 31. The rural sanitary districts included some parishes in other counties and some Devon parishes were in other counties' sanitary districts.

The situation in respect of highway administration and elementary education was too complex to be described in tabular form.

From 1889 to 1915 the geographical county was divided into four major local government systems – the three county boroughs of Plymouth, Devonport and Exeter, and the administrative county of Devon – but in 1914 the first two were merged with East Stonehouse to create a greater Plymouth. There were boundary changes in subsequent decades but no substantial change until 1968 when the local authorities of the largest urbanised area within the administrative county – Torquay, Paignton and Brixham – were merged to create the new county borough of Torbay. This situation lasted only until 1974 when all the county boroughs and the administrative county went out of existence, to be replaced by a non-metropolitan county containing all four systems.

Borough status and all associated structural questions were part of the jurisdiction of central government but the County Council was responsible for changes in urban and rural districts and parish government. Until 1929 it exercised its powers in a piecemeal reactive fashion, sitting in judgement on local proposals for boundary changes and promotions to urban status. Thus new urban districts were created at Kingsbridge (1893), Buckfastleigh (1894), Cockington (1894), Heavitree (1896), Ashburton (1898), Tavistock (1898), Holsworthy (1900), and Axminster (1915), whilst applications from St Budeaux (1897), Chudleigh (1897), Plymstock (1900), and others were turned down. Some urban districts disappeared into the county boroughs: St Thomas (1900) and Heavitree (1913) into Exeter, Compton Gifford (1896) and East Stonehouse (1914) into Plymouth. Torquay Non-County Borough gained St Marychurch (1900) and Cockington (1900).

In the 1930s the County Council had the duty to undertake a comprehensive review of its district and parish structure. The results were embodied in the *Devon Review Order, 1935*, which changed over 30 parish boundaries, demoted Bampton and Ivybridge from urban district status and merged Culmstock and Tiverton rural districts. In total the changes were not substantial and left Devon with a very familiar historic district and parish structure.

In the postwar period, apart from the creation of the new county borough of Torbay in 1968, there were only a few changes: voluntary demotions from town district status – Axminster (1953), Holsworthy (1964), Tavistock (1966) and South Molton (1967) – the division of Broadwoodwidger Rural District between Cornwall and Holsworthy Rural District (1966), and the modification of a small number of parish boundaries.

	non-county boroughs	urban districts	rural districts	parishes
1894	10	24	18	c. 450
1945	10	21	17	c. 400
1972	8	16	16	398

The reorganisation process of 1971–1974 reunited the parts of the Saxon-Norman county in a new Devon – the non-metropolitan or 'shire' county. It further abolished all very small non-county boroughs and urban districts and

medium-sized rural districts which were the striking feature of the administrative county, replacing them and the former county boroughs with a more
regular and simple pattern of ten districts. The three county boroughs went
through unchanged as new districts, five new areas were straightforward
mergers of adjacent town and rural districts, and only two involved the
division of an existing authority.

Once again the parish structure was virtually untouched so that, at the very
lowest level of Devon local government, many areas had boundaries that had
not been changed since time immemorial. However since then the work of the
Local Government Boundary Commission, established under the 1972 Act,
has produced a number of changes on a piecemeal basis.

The geography behind local government

Underlying this territorial pattern of authorities is a distribution of population whose reflection in the structure has been profoundly affected by
historical developments.

	Devon AC	Plymouth CB	Devonport CB	Exeter CB	Torbay CB
1891	455353	84248	54803	37404	—
1921	439996	└→ 210036 ←┘		59582	—
1951	514208	208017		75513	—
1971	407402	230406		88598	96293
1981	└————————————┴→ 952000 ←————————┴—————┘				

The population of the geographical county has been concentrated in two
main sectors of Devon. This may be illustrated by 1961 when its total
population was 823,000, but just over a quarter of a million lived in the Greater
Plymouth area and just over 300,000 were located in a narrow coastal strip and
hinterland, running west and south from the Dorset border to the estuary of
the Dart. About 60,000 lived around Barnstaple Bay and northwards along the
coast and the remaining 200,000 were scattered over a large area of central,
west and north Devon, with a salient in the South Hams, where towns of 4,000
population stood out as large centres and many areas looked to much smaller
villages.

Within the traditional area of English government known as 'Devon' there
is a wide range of social environments, often with diverse types in close
proximity. For instance some districts include both new suburbs and remote
parts of Dartmoor. Plymouth is one of the larger of English towns but not far
from it are some of the most remote and undeveloped parts of the country, as
well as medium and small towns, large and small villages and suburban
developments. Other districts include both a highly valued coast line and
inland areas of outstanding natural beauty. Cities and towns such as Exeter,
Tiverton and Barnstaple have a long history, whilst the Torbay area, apart
from Brixham, is a creation of the nineteenth century. Maritime, commercial
and leisure services, mining and quarrying, agriculture, light industry and
national defence have all been well-represented economic activities during

24

the last hundred years. Only the social environment associated with a concentration of heavy industry is lacking.

The County Council – the focus of this book – therefore has presided over a great variety of local environments within its boundaries and one of its tasks has been to reconcile the conflicting demands arising from these; to arbitrate between retirement and tourism, roads and moors, industry and plant life, and the past and future.

The Hundred Years: an Overview

During the hundred years of Devon County Council's existence national and local events have combined to mould its behaviour and structure and to join with the internal forces that all large organisations contain to create a general pattern of development which the centenary seeks to recognise and record. External forces are national when they occur in the country at large and are part of every locality's environment; they are local when they are specific to an area or small group of areas; forces are internal when they arise from the local authority itself as a miniature social and political system.

Some of the national forces making for change in all localities are those that are normally called simply 'social change'. They include urbanisation, the disappearance of traditional political families, the growth of leisure as an area of consumption, and the demand for territorial equality in the form of minimum standards of service provision throughout the country. More narrowly economic amongst these are the decline in landed estates and the modernisation of agriculture, the 'nationalisation' of industry and commerce, and, in the political sphere, the rise of the Labour Party, the increase in concern for efficiency and effectiveness in service provision, and the management movement in public administration. Others were more in the nature of events at the national level, occurring at particular periods; these include the expansion and redefinition of services by the Labour Government of 1945–50, and the process of re-allocation between types of local public body (1970–74), the organisation of the Conservative Party for action in local government in the late 1940s, periods when local government reform was a strong possibility (1945–49, 1958–65, 1969 onwards), the rates problem (1896, 1929, 1955–57, 1962–4), and Liberal 'revivals' (especially 1959–65).

Forces for change of a purely local nature tend to be more of a sort of 'event' or 'experience', such as the loss of territory (1900, 1913, 1914, 1940, 1950, 1966–68) or the various ratepayer and allied movements that have flashed across the local political heavens from time to time. But it must be remembered that national forces do not affect localities in a uniform manner; their 'strengths' are modified by the local social structure and diffusion processes often create time-lags in impact. Legal changes, for instance, may interact with social forces in ways peculiar to a given context.

This sort of interaction can be seen if consideration is given to economic change in Devon. Though Devon had once been a leading industrial county its position had been destroyed in the early nineteenth century. In the twentieth century agriculture, even after the 1947 Act, was not a satisfactory base for a local economy. Though the land in cultivation in Devon in the postwar period hardly changed the numbers employed dropped from 17,000 in 1954 to 6,300 in 1975. The number of farmers also dropped, though by about 30% as compared with 60% above. The increasing use of Devon as a retirement area also raised problems, especially as it conflicted to some extent with the growth of the holiday industry and tourism. All in all, society in Devon was seeking an economic role – would it become in H. G. Wells' terms the western suburb of a greater London (and presumably a thriving modern industrial area) or even more of a lower-income unbalanced society?

Since the late 1950s the County Council has openly sought a new role in the economic system for its territory by trying to modify the adverse effects of national and international economic change and exploiting natural local advantages. The authority is the repository of information about the whole area and the main source of evidence relating to economic decline and growth within its boundaries.

Pressures for change within the system of government

Local government in Devon responded slowly to many social changes in the twentieth century and the county, as part of the system of government, appeared to be old-fashioned, in some ways running behind other areas, particularly the more urbanised counties and larger towns and cities. Devon is not London and Torquay is not Birmingham.

To understand the evolution of the County Council in detail it is necessary to examine the relationships between decision-making within its 'walls' and changes that were taking place in the wider society. Unfortunately there is no space to document these in this book; all that can be done is to note the more significant national developments and form an impression of their delayed effects in the County. It should also be noted that Devon was occasionally amongst the leaders.

All public services have been affected by the attempted imposition of minimum standards of provision, partly through public demand and partly through legislative action, leading to the 'professionalisation of everything'. Every area has experienced pressure not to fall too far behind national averages and national standards. In the 1980s this is shown most clearly by the growth of leisure as a sphere of consumption.

All councils have been affected by the growth of a standard pattern of internal organisation for local authorities, with a greater stress on horizontal functions, and since the early 1960s described in the fashionable language of 'management'.

The disappearance of 'leisured classes' has led to attempts to improve the position of the layman in government, particularly in decentralised administration, by compensatory and enabling payments and supportive organisation. The 'nationalisation' of industry and commerce has replaced owners by managers, the decline of landed estates and the modernisation of agriculture has been associated with the withdrawal of traditional families from local public service, and urbanisation has provided the basis for working class involvement in local politics. Even in 1889 council members were aware of the monetary costs of local public service – they tried unsuccessfully to get

26

the railway companies to grant concessionary fares – and by 1988–89 it was necessary to compensate the vast majority of members for expenses incurred and income lost.

Devon and national politics

For most of the century the County Council has been in formal terms non partisan or 'controlled by independents'. But there is no evidence that in general elections voters are less partisan than elsewhere, and in fact turnout in Parliamentary elections tends generally to be higher in Devon than in much of the rest of the country. In national and European terms Devon is now overwhelmingly Conservative but this was not always the case. Until the First World War, and to some extent in the interwar period, Liberalism held its own, whilst the Labour Party made very slow progress within the County. The long-term consequence of this history has been that Conservatives and Liberals receive greater support and Labour less than in the country as a whole.

Of the factors that have exerted an influence over the whole period Conservatism has been a constant. The Conservative Party has always been strong in Devon and this has been reflected in the contribution its members have made to the County Council itself. The representation of the working classes and organised labour has increased slowly in the second half of the century but it still remains a negligible factor outside the cities of Plymouth and Exeter. The main variable factor has been Liberalism. The divisions within the centre of the British political spectrum have repeatedly affected county politics, as the Liberal Unionists, Coalition Liberals and National Liberals have broken away from the main Liberal Party, a phenomenon seen as recently as 1987–8 with the splits in the Alliance parties during the creation of the Social and Liberal Democratic Party. In contrast, the periodic revivals that Liberalism has experienced at national level have also been reflected at county level.

Devon's economic history

Economic and social changes are reflected in local population history. Many parts of Devon were areas of de-industrialisation after 1800, and though total population grew through the period it was at a much slower rate than in the country as a whole – and some areas experienced a decline in absolute numbers. From the last quarter of the nineteenth century until the Second World War agriculture was always a fragile economic activity, which generally did not support high incomes for those working in it. To strengthen the employment base of the County individuals have sought to exploit its natural advantages by developing tourism as an economic activity and encouraging outsiders to retire to the area.

In addition to agriculture some of the other main economic activities are rightly regarded as fragile. Maritime activities, including trade, are directly affected by the international economic climate and indirectly by changes in the distribution of national population and internal communications. Fishing is like agriculture – at the mercy of national and supra-national political institutions. The extractive industries everywhere tend to suffer very severely from the 'downs' of the trade cycle. National defence is no longer a closely guarded internal monopoly; it is also threatened by reductions in international tension. Tourism and the holiday industry depend in part on exchange rates and are damaged by adverse publicity about environmental hazards. Even the 'retirement' industry can be weakened by high rates of inflation which undermine the value of savings and private pensions.

Some time in the late 1950s or early 1960s Devon began to experience renewed population growth in many parts. This is a sign of economic growth and development which has changed everyone's perspective on the economic future of the County. The progress, however, is not evenly distributed throughout the area and some parts still need extensive help from central government and the European Community. Recent growth seems connected with improvements in the system of communications with the rest of the country and further developments, such as the North Devon link road and the connection of Plymouth with the European mainland, may help to increase the geographical spread of prosperity. The crucial issue, however, is the improvement of connections between the County and the Channel Tunnel, something that is of concern to every county outside the South-East.

For most of the century of its existence the County Council has faced the problems of a declining or stagnant economy. It still experiences these in some parts of its territory but it is also facing the development problems posed by the efforts of national firms and multi-national corporations to expand their operations within its boundaries. The County Council has become Janus-faced; it has to follow the dual strategy of stressing on the one hand the relative deprivation of the north and west and the inner areas of Plymouth, the weakness of a livestock-based agriculture, the vulnerability of tourism and the problems of an ageing population, and on the other hand the economic advantages and potential of the County for the industries of the future. No one wants to repeat the mistakes of the past, when marginal firms and weak industries were attracted to the area; for the County Council the economic future is seen as coming from Japan and America, via the 'high-tec' science-based industries.

Devon and the rest of the South West

Part of Devon's history lies with the other counties of the South West. The peninsular nature of the South West has led to it being regarded as a distinct region by both society in general and the government itself. Devon is always joined with Cornwall when regions are created by public and private organisations. It has close connections with west and south west Somerset and west Dorset, but the policy of combining it with the 'West of England' district and other areas to the north and east in a Greater South West is not popular with local political and administrative leaders.

From a county-centred perspective the boundaries of Devon have contributed to its stability over time. Compared with other parts of the country Devon has had no territorial disputes with its neighbours, except over relatively small pieces of land – and most of these have been solved in piecemeal fashion during the last hundred years. Co-operation with Cornwall is straightforward in principle but its other two neighbours are drawn towards the large urban areas on their other borders – Somerset to Bristol and Dorset to Bournemouth and Southampton-Portsmouth.

The one issue that unites the four counties more than any other is the problem of transportation. Communications between Cornwall and the rest of the country cannot be improved unless those of Devon, Somerset and Dorset are also modernised. The creation of the motorway system was an earlier influence on all of them; now the Channel Tunnel, as mentioned above, has become the focus of regional thinking.

Devon and its urban areas

Though few complications arise from the County's external boundaries the same is not true of its internal socio-geographical patterns. Though the popular image of Devon is of an area of villages and small seaside towns in fact it contains one large and two medium-sized urban areas, and these between them contain over half the County's population. During most of the period the two longest-established urban areas – Exeter and Plymouth – were outside the jurisdiction of the County Council, and the other – Torbay – achieved that status for a very short period, in fact 1968–74.

Some of the social and organisational stability of the pre-1974 County Council must be attributed to the removal of the urban political systems from its territory. The repeated transfer of the growing suburbs to the county boroughs, as the major urban areas experienced demands for consolidation into a single authority (to minimise 'free-riding', to exploit economies of scale and to enhance area-wide action and community feeling), prevented new political forces from obtaining a foothold on the County Council.

Thus Exeter took in the adjacent urban districts of St Thomas (1900) and Heavitree (1913), and added suburban parishes in 1940 and 1966. The present city of Plymouth started as 'the three towns' – the county boroughs of Devonport and Plymouth with the urban district of East Stonehouse. The original Plymouth had gained some territory from the county in the first twenty years of the system but the major change was the consolidation of the three as a new county borough in 1914. Since that time it has acquired suburban parishes to the north and east, the last occasion being in 1967.

The Torbay area was a significant part of the administrative county for most of its history. Torquay rose from being a number of seaside villages in 1801, through local board to non-county borough status in 1892. It acted as the focus for urban consolidation in its hinterland. At the same time its neighbouring parish of Paignton progressed to urban district status in 1894, as did the separate small port of Brixham. Until the 1950s the 'separateness' of the three areas was taken for granted but the 1958 Act gave urban conglomerations an incentive to forget their differences and seek promotion to county borough status. The Torbay area, not without stumbling, managed to achieve this in 1968, making Devon County Council a significantly more rural authority.

Outside Torbay, towns of over fifteen thousand inhabitants were regarded as major urban areas. Devon was therefore similar to many other 'peripheral' areas and contrasted very markedly with counties such as Middlesex, Surrey, Kent and Essex.

Local government reorganisation in 1971–74 restored the Saxon-Norman boundaries of Devon by abolishing 'county' status for the three boroughs so that the social structure of the local government county is now much more urban in aggregate than ever before. The effect of reorganisation was dramatic in relation to the County Council as a local authority. The changes of its first eighty years were largely evolutionary but 1974 witnessed a dramatic discontinuity in county politics consequent on the merging of the political systems of the administrative county and three county boroughs.

The First County Council in Devon

Part of the opposition to the creation of county councils came from those who took a very pessimistic view of the viability of the electoral process in relation to county-wide authorities. The 'doomsday' prophets took the view that the traditional county leadership would not seek election and there was no-one else to take its place. County councils would fail because no-one would be found able and willing to serve on them.

In the case of Devon this view was disproved by events. The costs in time and money were particularly onerous because of its large area and the great distances of some parts from the county town, Exeter, yet from the very beginning the Council attracted the active support of both old and new 'elites'. In fact the new institution attracted the support of Devon's national political leaders – peers of the realm and members of the House of Commons – and several were frequent lecturers on the subject of local government reform within the County.

The active recruitment process began almost before the royal assent had been given on August 13th, 1888. By the beginning of September likely candidates were being mentioned for several areas and as autumn passed the list grew rapidly longer. There were widespread expectations that the leaders of Quarter Sessions would seek election – and often be unopposed – and that others would join the process. Lists of possible and probable candidates for each division were regularly published in the local press and it was very clear that at least Devon County Council would not fail because of a lack of support from public-spirited individuals.

A study of the recruitment process reveals a strong social and political basis for the new authority. First, many of the 'incumbents' – those who had been active in quarter sessions – were real potential candidates and then actual candidates. Secondly, despite many reservations about party politics in county government, the parties, including Liberal Unionists as a separate group, took an interest in the process. Partisanship appeared in several guises (though not the organisational form found today in strong party authorities): as straight party conflict, as bipartisanship, as transpartisanship, as intra-party conflict and as non-partisanship. Thirdly, religious divisions, often related to party affiliation, were widely regarded as relevant to electoral choice. Methodists and churchmen were often opposed in competition for a seat on the council. There were also class conflicts in some areas, particularly between agriculture and industry or commerce in economically mixed areas, and between tenants and landowners in rural areas.

It was also widely recognised that a division needed strong representation at county level and candidatures were discussed in village, town and poor law union terms. Factors such as experience in public affairs, social standing, personal resources and personal qualities were canvassed as relevant to the choice of 'ambassador' to the county council chamber. An examination of both unsuccessful and successful candidates reveals that the new authority did very well in these respects.

The pessimists were wrong and whatever faults the County Council may have had they did not result from a failure to attract the support of county society. In fact, from its earliest days Devon County Council succeeded in gaining the long-term, generally permanent, loyalty of those elected to it. Like every formal organisation the County Council had some short-service councillors and aldermen, whose quick departure did not necessarily mean a rejection of the authority, but these were greatly outnumbered by individuals who served for more than a decade and often until death terminated their membership.

The early meetings of the County Council

The arrangements for electing the first county councils were laid down in some detail. The administrative process for drawing up the register of electors and creating county electoral divisions was in the hands of the Clerk of the Peace and the Sheriff, and had to be completed by the beginning of 1889. The first elections had to be held on or after January 14th and the newly elected members had to meet as the provisional council on the second Thursday after polling day. The first meeting was to be organisational, electing a temporary chairman and aldermen, then adjourning to a second meeting to which the latter would also be called. During February and March the provisional council met to create its own decision-making structures and processes, and to co-ordinate with Quarter Sessions a smooth takeover of county functions. On the first of April, 1889, Devon County Council came into full formal existence and has continued as a recognisable part of the English system of local government to the present day.

In taking over functions and services from Quarter Sessions the County Council also took over staff and financial arrangements. It began with the Clerk of the Peace as Clerk to the County Council and responsible as an individual for his subordinate staff. The treasurer was the manager of the National Provincial Bank guaranteed by sureties from its senior officers and the Council also inherited a stock of substantial buildings in which major responsibilities were discharged. The Council's main organisational task was to frame its own standing orders and create a committee system through which members could carry out their functions.

Partly because it was a new body and partly because the law was not as helpful, in a managerial sense, as it might have been, the County Council at first had to hold meetings more frequently and irregularly than became the norm after a few years. From the very start it recognised the existence of lower level authorities within its boundaries and based many of its administrative arrangements on them. Council members also undertook specific tasks which it would now be the responsibility of officers to initiate and carry through their main stages.

In the first six years of its existence individual members mentioned their original misgivings about its viability but all concluded that that they had not been realised. The County Council established itself as an organisation and, as with other county councils, before the end of the nineteenth century had gained several new services: technical instruction, isolation hospitals, small-holdings, fertilisers and feeding stuffs, light railways, and the treatment of alcoholism. Devon had also raised an issue of local importance which has continued until the present-day – the management of the Forest of Dartmoor and the role of 'outside' bodies such as the Duchy of Cornwall and the War Department.

Main Developments, 1889–1989

What marked the history of the County Council until reorganisation in 1973–1974 was the dominance of evolutionary processes which reflected the twin and joint impact of national events and the local environment. There were few happenings that did not have some consequences for Devon but their impact was worked out for the most part gradually and without dramatic crises and discontinuities. As a local authority Devon in 1973 was very different from what it had been in 1889 but it was impossible to say when the transitions took place. As a local political system the changes had been even more impercep-tible and the historian is hard put to identify any quantitatively significant developments.

The two world wars, however, do form dividing periods in the history of the County Council. The wartime years are themselves distinct but on a macroscopic view they belong more to the periods before the start than to those after the end of the conflicts.

In its early years the County Council was a relatively small organisation. It discharged many of its functions through other public agencies and had a very small permanent staff. It was to a considerable extent a supervisory or tutelage authority. Most national developments, however, after 1889 tended to increase the role of the County Council, particularly in the sphere of direct service provision. The first major event was the founding of the modern system of education by the Education Act, 1902. This changed the scale of financial operations of the Council and gave it a major administrative department of its own. This created pressure for the rationalisation of common services and the employment of full-time staff in other spheres. The expansion of staff and departmental organisation brought eventually and reluctantly unions, national pay agreements and superannuation to the County.

However the supervisory role remained, especially in relation to areas, boundaries, elections, rating and by-laws of the reformed lower-tier authorities brought into existence by the 1894 Act. The administration of justice and the police service were also examples of a sphere for which the County Council was partly responsible but in which it did not generally act directly. The county health services were also in practice under the direct control of large institutions with boards of management as were the further education colleges. Default powers in relation to environmental health were always in the background and occasionally awkward situations arose with individual districts who had to be reported to central government.

In the first period roads, bridges, weights and measures, and agriculture occupied a considerable part of the County Council's attention. Once education had been reorganised in 1902 it became the major county service, a role which has been maintained to this day. The major local issue was Dartmoor – its status, control and future. The problems that it generated during this period were beyond the capacity of the County Council of the time to solve; only changes in national legislation could make a difference in this respect.

Between the wars

During the second period most County Council activities expanded but still in general gradually, with just the occasional minor upset or 'crisis'. In the field of welfare and personal health the process created a patchwork of separate services for distinct client groups. The difficulties of agriculture turned the Council's attention towards the economic base of the area, but periodic national financial crises created pressure for local measures of economy. Unionisation increased with an increasing 'nationalisation' of local government employment. The elected membership changed slowly but except for the virtual disappearance of peers of the realm there was a sense of continuity going back to the early years of the century. The factors identified as influencing the elections to the first county council continued to play a part in the recruitment process.

The Second World War had a more substantial influence on county government. Many of the ordinary processes of government were suspended and avowedly temporary changes introduced. The end of hostilities in Europe led to moves designed to return the system to normality. When elections were resumed in 1946 all councillors and half the aldermen had to seek re-election. There had been many changes since 1937: extension of the local franchise, war damage and population change, a Labour victory in the 1945 General Election, and Labour gains in borough elections in November, 1945. General political uncertainty was at its greatest since 1889 and no-one could be sure that the old patterns had survived.

After the Second World war

The Devon of 1945 appeared to exhibit a style of local government which was passing or had passed in other areas. First, partisanship was almost entirely absent from elections outside the two county boroughs. The drives that the Labour Party made in other counties during the inter-war years had no

33

counterpart in the administrative county of Devon and there was little substantial overt Liberal-Conservative conflict. The election of eight Labour candidates to the county council in 1946 was a high point never achieved again until reorganisation; and the smattering of seats won in the larger districts tended also to decline by the end of the decade. At national level the Conservative Party organised itself for greater intervention in local government during 1947–49 but this had virtually no effect on Devon County Council elections and organisation. In some parts of Devon from time to time there were short-lived local political movements. The late 1950s saw a Liberal revival in some areas and this was continued into the 1960s, being followed in some places by meteoric ratepayers movements.

Secondly, the social leaders who had dominated the first English county councils had maintained their position in Devon for far longer than in many other counties for which there is substantial evidence. In 1945 Devon County Council was still a very traditional body in social composition. Many of the names were familiar to students of Devon history, being identical in many cases with those of Victorian members. Many individual council members belonged to the 'political families' of the county and many had entered local government during an earlier age and had grown old in its service. The specific occupations were revealing; some even declared an hereditary title as their electoral description. The landed interest was well represented as were professions and substantial local businesses. The significance of land and the traditional families is probably under-stated because another category – retired military and naval personnel – also included individuals who properly belonged to this group.

Thirdly, the management structure of councils was only just beginning to be professionalised and systematised. The County Council had very few chief officers and throughout the area the employment of part-timers, 'consultants' and 'Pooh-Bahs' was common in the higher levels of the local government officer structure. The postwar period saw a rapid strengthening of the administrative leadership of councils throughout the county.

Fourthly, the pattern of districts and parishes within Devon's boundaries had not been modernised during the 1930s when many counties carried through fairly extensive reviews as required by the legislation of 1929 and 1933. A few minute districts disappeared but the overall picture would have been familiar to those who had known it in 1901. The failure or refusal to reform the district structure of the county is a recurrent theme of the postwar period. The fact that Devon had so many small districts within its boundaries has considerable significance for the understanding of the general stability of the area.

The Labour Governments of 1945 to 1951 had a decisive effect on the development of county government. The scale of change in services contrasted strongly with the gradualism of most other five- or ten-year periods. From being a tutelage authority with gradually increasing direct service responsibilities the County Council jumped to being a major pillar of the welfare state (with its personal non-hospital health services and services for children and the aged), the main controller of spatial development, and the leading provider of protective services. The role of education expanded and only agriculture declined in importance for the Council, whilst hospitals were lost to local government everywhere.

The result was a transformation of the County Council into a leading local authority. As the services given to it immediately after the war tended to grow in importance during the next two decades the upper tier became more and more significant year by year. Not until 1973 was the process reversed.

During the whole of this period local authorities as individuals shared only a few common experiences relevant to local democracy – in 1948 they were given a limited power to pay expenses and allowances to their members, in 1969 the franchise was extended and party labels were permitted on the ballot paper, and for a brief period in 1970–71 the number of qualifications for election was reduced before being increased beyond the traditional range.

The approach to reorganisation

It is difficult at this distance in time to appreciate the transformation of the dominant perspectives on local government between 1958 and 1972. The period 1958 to 1965 was shaped by the work of the Local Government Commission for England. The whole process, which included several stages and other actors as well as the Commission, was fragmented, reactive and long-drawn out, and though in Devon it produced expansions of Exeter and Plymouth and the creation of Torbay County Borough, it became increasingly regarded as not relevant to the main problems of local government and the Commission eventually more or less committed suicide.

Three major enquiries were instituted in the mid–1960s; the Maud Committee on the management of local government (1964–1967), the Mallaby Committee on the staffing of local government (1964–1967), and the Redcliffe-Maud Royal Commission on the structure of local government (1966–1969). The impact of the first two was not dramatic in Devon or indeed anywhere but they gave an impetus to the management movement so that within a very short time the traditional language of administration and co-ordination had been replaced by the vocabulary of management, policy and planning. From the mid–1960s onwards the internal organisation of the County Council moved significantly away from the traditional pattern towards a management-oriented system. The Bains Report in 1972, coming just before the implementation of reorganisation, gave a final push in the direction of the new orthodoxy of corporate planning, the chief executive system, chief officers' group, rationalised committee structures, delegation down the hierarchy and the use of management services.

The period was brought to an end by the *Local Government Act, 1972*, which created a new set of authorities and cancelled the elections for existing authorities which would have been held in 1973 (and of course subsequent years). In 1974, therefore, the local political system of traditional Devon disappeared through local government reform.

In territorial terms Devon survived this period because the Labour Government was defeated in the 1970 General Election. Proposals for reform arising from the Redcliffe-Maud Commission would have created 'unitary authorities' in Devon and Cornwall with the traditional counties as areas of local government disappearing altogether. The Labour Government adopted the Majority's scheme but was defeated before the White Paper could be turned into law. The Conservative Government rejected 'unitary' authorities in favour of a two-tier system. Though the changes that were implemented were radical in the six provincial conurbations, four other areas of England and parts of Wales, Devon emerged as a non-metropolitan or 'shire' county by the simple process of merging the three county boroughs with the administrative county, thus restoring the Saxon-Norman boundaries with only very small exceptions.

Perhaps local government reorganisation and associated legal changes came at just the right time for the reputation of the old Devon County Council. Though the system had evolved over eighty years and had survived very difficult times in mid-century, there were signs that the system was changing in directions that suggested that in the long run it was doomed.

The difficulties were seen first in the recruitment system. There was a hint that partisanship was increasing towards the end of the period in certain urban areas and that this would eventually lead to even less stable delegations from those areas, if national party fortunes continued to vary in the way that was experienced in the last eight years of the system. There were also signs that the supply of candidates was changing in that there were fewer young people able to offer the time needed for county council work, so that more old people featured amongst the candidates and this boded ill for the creation of cohorts of long service members. The above are just hints but they fit in well with what is believed to have occurred in the social structure at large – namely the passing away of a leisured or semi-leisured class.

The aldermanic system also suggested that changes were taking place in the membership of the council. As time progressed the degree of consensus seemed to decline and electoral behaviour at aldermanic elections indicated that members were less pre-socialised and less agreed about organisational decisions. First, voters were more willing to withdraw votes from incumbents so that the spread of votes between highest and lowest increased and the vote of the least popular eventually fell to a level that led to failure to be re-elected. The withdrawal of votes from incumbents increased markedly in the 1950s, dropped back in 1964, but reached an unprecedented level in 1968. Candidature patterns for 'vacancies' suggested the same sort of development. Indices of candidature showed a tendency to increase irregularly as time passed, but more significantly the proportion of the council voting for the winning candidate declined, also irregularly. In fact in the later period several ties occurred which necessitated the use of the chairman's casting vote, and other votes were very close.

Population growth began to increase in parts of Devon after 1961; it is hard to believe that had not reorganisation come there would eventually have had to be a major redistricting of the county electoral divisions. This would have had two effects; first, an effect on continuity because 'clean sweep' elections are always occasions for 'opting-out' of legislatures, and second, a long term effect on the balance between relatively stable and unstable divisions.

The *Local Government Act, 1972*, its associated regulations and the processes it set in motion caused a sharp break in the evolution of county government in

Devon. The merging of the county boroughs with the administrative county produced a local authority area that was more urban than Devon had ever experienced. At the same time many rural areas and small towns were undergoing economic change which was reducing the importance of agriculture to local society. Reorganisation also coincided with changing philosophies of public sector management and with the very different national financial climate forced on the United Kingdom by the global economic system.

After reorganisation

When reorganisation came it brought dramatic changes in the political system of the county council. The merger with the large urban areas produced a drive for partisanship throughout the county and only in north and west Devon did independents fight off the (mainly) Conservative challenge. The introduction of attendance allowances in place of the totally inadequate and inappropriate loss of earnings system meant in principle that more people were able to serve at county level. The aldermanic system – one of the mainstays of the status system of the council and a substantial contributor to continuity of member-ship – was abolished. The new system of districts contained no small authorities and in three cases down-graded county boroughs. A sign of the times was the rise in the proportion of female candidates and members. Women averaged 8% of all postwar candidates and 10% for the last three ordinary elections before reorganisation but the 1973 elections produced 22.4% female candidates and a council membership of 18% female.

The most significant aspect of reorganisation in Devon was the doubling of the population of the County through its acquisition of Exeter, Plymouth and Torbay. District sizes increased dramatically as the number of areas was reduced to ten, and the multitude of minute and small town and rural districts that were characteristic of the administrative county disappeared as principal authorities. The average size of county electoral divisions doubled and an effort was made to create greater equality between areas in terms of numbers of electors. But above all the party politics of the major urban areas was carried to the rest of the county by the deliberate action of the local branches of the main national parties. Overnight Devon passed from being genuinely non-partisan to a fully organised party system.

The first elections to the new council were held in April, 1973. Electoral behaviour changed dramatically. For the 98 seats the Conservative Party nominated 94 candidates, the Labour Party 93, and the Liberals 50. As there were also 44 'others' the total number of candidates was 281. At least 34 were 'carpet-baggers', having no connection with the division they contested, and many of the others must have been 'defeatists', that is, candidates standing to make sure that their party is represented and the seat contested. Few were newcomers to Devon local government, nearly fifty being members of the previous county council and nearly eighty being members of a county borough council. The result was seen in a changed pattern of candidatures: in the single member divisions, whereas three candidates had been rare and four or five almost unknown, three-way or more contests were the rule.

The Conservative Party won an absolute majority of seats – 54 out of 98 – and the Labour Party 20, 12 of which were in Plymouth, 4 in Exeter, 2 in Torbay and 2 in Newton Abbot. In the north and west Liberals and 'others' did well and overall totalled 11 and 13 respectively. Many of the independents were members of the old Council. The 'transfer' rate (21/51) between old and new was in fact fairly high, in the light of the small number of divisions in what had been the administrative county.

Because of changes in the law and practice relating to the self description of it is not so easy to gather information about the occupations of candidates and elected members. Most of the probable changes, however, must be attributed to the 'delegations' from Plymouth and Exeter.

From 1973 to 1985 the Conservative Group on the Council controlled the representative side of organisation and decision-making, running the system as a majority party 'administration' on Westminster lines. Choice of presiding officer, committee chairmanships and major policy decisions were in the hands of the Conservatives, the 'opposition' was divided into three separate groups and, particularly between 1977 and 1981, was extremely weak in numerical terms.

The Council's political system changed dramatically at the 1985 ordinary elections. Although they remained the largest group the Conservatives lost their overall majority and were replaced by the Alliance as the 'administration'. This relied on the tacit support of the small Labour Group but otherwise acted as the governing group on the Council, providing the leader, the presiding officer and committee chairmen.

After two years the informal coalition fell apart because the Labour Group had become increasingly critical of some Alliance policies and the Council entered a very difficult period when none of the groups would or could take the leadership roles that the system contains. Eventually a *modus vivendi* was evolved between all the major groups but the merger of the two parties forming the Alliance led to the 'hiving-off' of the Owenite Social Democratic Party.

A four-party situation thus obtains in the last few months of the first hundred years of Devon County Council. Everyone awaits the next ordinary elections which will take place in May, 1989, and which may provide a solution to some of the political problems facing the authority.

4

THE ORGANISATION OF THE COUNTY COUNCIL

All British local authorities have to create a dual-sided organisation, which provides for the discharge of the respective roles of elected representatives and appointed officials. One dimension consists of the characteristic institutions for council members and the other the structures in which employees work. The internal organisation of each local authority is complex because not only does it have two separate dimensions but each must play a part in decision-making, individuals and groups within each must interact with their counterparts within the other, and both must deal with the world outside the local authority.

It is easy to lose sight of the fact that the individual local authority has a working system which embraces all participants and reaches out into society at large. Devon County Council was and is not just a collection of individuals and groups fortuitously brought together but a social system with political and administrative functions to which each part made and makes characteristic contributions. It is also easy to lose sight of the fact that all social organisations change with the passage of time. In the case of large-scale organisations the changes tend to make the system more formal and 'institutionalised': clearer boundaries between the organisation and the rest of society, more precisely differentiated roles within it, and 'universalised' rules for organisational decisions create a local 'constitution' with its own conventions, its characteristic patterns of behaviour and its own culture. The reverse also occasionally happens when organisations become less formal and 'de-institutionalised'. Flexible 'conventions' and intangible culture may crumble under the impact of developments in the rest of society; patterns of behaviour may change and the organisation will then present a different picture to the outside world.

In the case of Devon County Council the development of the committee system, the departmental structure and employer-employee relations – personnel management in the widest sense – over the hundred years embodies evolutionary processes which have turned a small organisation acting mainly through other public and private bodies into a major self-contained executive agency with a large staff. Before the Second World War the speed of change was slow but in two periods – 1945–50 and 1965–74 – considerable re-structuring took place; this reflected in the first period the accession of major new responsibilities as a result of implementation of the Labour Government's policies, and in the second the rapid acceptance of 'management' as the key organisational principle for a local authority.

Prior to 1972 there were short episodes of disarray and disruptive controversy but these turned out to be no more than interruptions of the long-term process of 'institutionalisation' and 'modernisation'. During the process of reorganisation there were a number of sources of difficulty in creating the new local authority but two factors reduced the significance of these. The first was the outcome of the 1973 ordinary election which created a Conservative overall majority on the Council and the second was the widespread acceptance of the 'philosophy of management' that had developed in the local government world in the previous decade and which was embodied in the Bains Report of 1972.

The Overall Pattern

By 1960 there had emerged in Britain a general consensus about how the modern local authority should be structured. The organisation of elected members can be summarised as 'councillors everywhere'. They were present at council, committee and subcommittee meetings, at both headquarters and area levels; they took their turn on visiting committees, working parties and study groups; they divided up the positions on boards of governors and management committees; they represented their authority on joint boards, joint committees and private organisations. In partisan authorities council members also had a system of institutions which mirrored in part the formal structure of the authority as set out above: an executive committee or leadership group, a 'caucus' or meeting of all party members, 'caucuses' of committee members, and party officers, including leader and 'whip'.

The organisation of council employees involved 'officers everywhere' as only in strongly partisan authorities did council members meet formally without some officials being present. But in addition employee structures invariably involved a tension and conflict between 'bureaucracy' and 'professionalism'. The 'bureaucratic' factor arose because each department was a formal organisation in its own right, stressing hierarchy, clearly defined duties, and 'knowing by doing'. The 'professional' factor arose because each department contained one or more professions, stressing equality, problem-solving and academic expertise. The tension between the two was apparent in 'life chances' (recruitment, training, promotion, remuneration and working conditions) and in 'authority' – 'men' versus 'ideas'. Thus though the typical employee structures – headquarters, area offices, satellites, depots, and 'associates' – were in principle common to all services, professionals tended to prefer flexible and egalitarian organisational forms rather than rigid and hierarchical ones – teams rather than divisions, working parties rather than sections, case conferences rather than sub-sections.

It was fortunate for Devon that the Bains 'model' existed in 1973 because the new County's organisation had to be created and imposed on four different administrative systems. The pattern of chief executive, policy committee with sub-committees, a small number of specialist standing committees and a number of 'directors' heading major groups of related services and functions, is familiar to the student of local government reorganisation. What marked Devon out from many of the rest was the thoroughness with which it adopted the principle of systematic area organisation, which plays a small part in Bains, for the organisation of the work of both councillors and officers.

In the rest of this chapter a brief look is taken at the development of each of the main elements in the County Council's organisation in order to set the scene for the analysis of leadership and some general aspects of the working of the system.

Council Meetings

The first meeting of the Council proper, after three meetings as a provisional council, was on April 1st, 1889. From and including that date there were 30 meetings up to and including December, 1892, followed by an average of 5 a year until 1899 when the system settled down to the four quarterly meetings supplemented by the rare extra meeting for a special purpose. After the Second World War it became the practice to hold a special budget meeting in February at which the main business was setting the rate for the coming year. After reorganisation the Council met more frequently, in fact on a bi-monthly basis.

The starting and finishing times have always proved something of a problem and there have been frequent changes. The difficulty is that if the meeting starts too early the members representing distant divisions cannot get to it on time and if it starts too late they often have to leave before the end of business has been reached. In order to try to reconcile these conflicting demands the starting time has ranged from 10.30 a.m. to 2.30 p.m. No formal account is available about when council meetings have ended and the lists of attenders at the beginning of the minutes record only the fact that an individual has been present in the Council Chamber for at least some of the time. There were repeated decisions in the early years to publish attendance records but if these were actually compiled they do not seem to have survived. Once an element of payment to members was introduced, however, it was necessary for the Council's staff to keep a much more systematic record of members' participation.

The place of meeting has always been Exeter. Until the purpose-built County Hall on Topsham Road was opened the full Council met in the Castle, which served Quarter Sessions and still contains the County's courts. There were many complaints about the inadequacy of the 'Nisi Prius' court and a proposal for a new county council building was considered, but rejected in favour of improvements to the Castle, in 1893. It was not until 1963 that a change was made; the present County Hall contains a continental-style semi-circular chamber with seats for every member which contrasts with the adversary pattern of the House of Commons. However complaints continued from press and public about the acoustics of the chamber and several attempts have been made to improve audibility.

Chief officers and secretarial staff are normally present at council meetings but apart from the Clerk to the Council they do not make a formal contribution, though notes used to be passed to committee chairmen and messages whispered when this was possible. Others present include local journalists, and the full Council meeting has usually had extensive coverage in the local press. A varying number of members of the public attend meetings, and in recent years there have been occasional disruptions by aggrieved interests and a growth of public lobbying before and during meetings.

For most of the hundred years the vast majority of items of business have gone through 'on the nod' as part of extensive committee reports circulated in advance to members. In the very early years there was a tendency for motions to be put down but withdrawn before debate, but when the system settled down business introduced in this manner became rare. Most discussion arose from items in the committee reports, often because non-committee members disagreed with the 'specialists' or because a minority on the committee wished to appeal against a decision of the majority.

Since reorganisation the formal pattern remains the same, in the sense that committee reports form the basis of the agenda and business to be transacted. But during the period of Conservative dominance most internal committee and party differences were sorted out before the public meeting of the Council so that the full Council took on the appearance of party confrontation rather than the diffuse and formless conflict of the non-partisan system. Since the resignation of the Alliance 'administration' in 1987 the situation has acquired an unpredictability that it never experienced even in the earliest years when the 'conventions' of the local constitution were being established.

One type of business that is common to all periods is that which involves ceremony and ritual. Council meetings are occasions for expressing pleasure and sadness at events within and outside the local authority. Council meetings are also necessary for certain types of organisational matters, such as the notification of resignations of members and the adoption of certain types of resolution.

Council Members and Elections

Of all aspects of the operation of a local authority the work of council members is the easiest to describe and the hardest to analyse. The contributions of elections, the council meeting and the committee system to overall decision-making defy simple assessment because these elements tend to be constants for long periods. Their influence is pervasive rather than episodic and discrete. The influence of elections is the most difficult to assess. They connect the social and political processes of the community to the council processes which ultimately issue in decision-making which in its turn affects the community. But they do this through the persons of individual men and women who actually serve on the council.

The participation of individuals

British local authorities make heavy demands on the individuals who serve on them. In the case of Devon the hundred years have demanded an 'elected manpower' contribution of almost 10,500 'council service years', nearly 9,000 before reorganisation and 1,500 since then. In the pre-1974 system the total time was divided between about 720 individuals, making an average of 12. 5 years each, whilst in the new system the 'years' have been divided between about 225 individuals, making an average of 6.67 years each.

Contributions have been unequal. Some individuals in the traditional system served for only a few weeks or months, whilst others were members for thirty or forty years. Some members in the new system have held office for only a short time but a few have served the maximum so far of sixteen years.

Service on a council is not just a matter of turning up for council meetings; the organisational system described above makes demands on individuals for participation in committees, sub-committees and management boards, and as representatives on or delegates to other bodies. Council members also often participate in other public bodies, including other local authorities, the machinery of justice and local 'quangos'. Though the latter is not legally necessary a system in which individuals were county council members only would be very different from the ones that have operated in Devon.

Because of the complexity and obscurity of many aspects of participation it is not possible to give even approximate figures for the total time spent on public and public-related business by county council members. To do so requires information about frequency, duration, travelling time and actual attendance at meetings. The description of the County Council's organisational structure below, however, indicates the most important sources of demands on the time of members.

Electoral Systems and Electoral Behaviour

County Council elections have always been supposed to be based entirely on single-member electoral divisions but in 1889 and in 1973 the full administrative arrangements could not be made in time so that multi-member constituencies were found in some areas, particularly the large urban areas – Torquay, East Stonehouse, and Tiverton in 1889, Plymouth and Exeter in 1973–1981. Overwhelmingly, however, divisions have returned one member at each election.

The map of electoral divisions established for the 1889 elections proved to be remarkably stable. Occasionally divisions disappeared because of loss of territory to the county boroughs – St Thomas 1900, Heavitree 1913, East Stonehouse 1914, Tamerton Foliot 1950, and those in Torbay and in the suburbs of Exeter and Plymouth in 1966–68. The urban area of Newton Abbot gained an extra seat in 1910, as did Exmouth and Paignton in 1925. The most substantial redrawing of county constituency boundaries was for the 1937 election, but even then most of the areas were unaffected. The urban and

First Chairman of the Council, Baron Clinton 1889–1901

First Clerk of the Council, Henry Michelmore 1889–1912

CHAIRMEN OF THE COUNCIL 1901–1989

The Earl of Morley 1901–1904

Earl Fortescue 1904–1916

Sir Henry Hepburn 1916

Sir Henry Lopes 1916–1937

Sir John Daw 1938–1946

Sir John Shelley 1946–1955

Sir George Hayter-Hames 1955–1965

John Day 1965–1966

Gerald Whitmarsh CBE 1966–1971   *Col. Eric Palmer CBE 1971–1973*

Charles Ansell 1973–1977   *Samuel Sargent 1977–1978*

Leslie Goodrich OBE 1978–1981

George Creber CBE 1981–1985

Douglas Potter 1985–1986

William Evans 1986–1987

Mrs Ena Stacey MBE 1987–1988

Arnold Sayers CBE 1988–1989

The Castle, Exeter, first home of Devon County Council

An aerial view of County hall, Exeter (Express & Echo, Exeter)

The Council Chamber at County Hall, Exeter during a Council meeting (1978)

UNDER TEN PREMIERS

Tribute To Mr. G. Lambert, M.P.

MESSAGE FROM MR. LLOYD GEORGE

Honoured At Crediton Dinner

NEARLY half a century's public service by the Right Hon. George Lambert, M.P., was recognized in a complimentary dinner to the Hon. Member and Mrs. Lambert, at the Ship Hotel, Crediton, last night.

Though organized under the auspices of the Liberal Association of South Molton Division, which Mr. Lambert has represented in Parliament for most of that period, the tribute was joined in by other prominent persons, irrespective of party.

Special interest attached to a message from Mr. D. Lloyd George, one of the ten Prime Ministers under whom Mr. Lambert has served.

Mr. Lambert entered public life at the age of 21 as a member of the old Okehampton Board of Guardians. He became county councillor for North Tawton Division, and then, over 40 years ago, was returned to the House of Commons for the South Molton Division. Mr. Lambert, then the youngest M.P., is the second oldest continuously sitting Member to Mr Lloyd George, and would be the oldest but for a temporary break commencing in 1924.

Long service – George Lambert, who completed 63 years as a County Councillor

End of an era – County Council members who attended the final meeting in 1973, before the establishment of the post-reorganisation County Council, pictured with their Chairman, Col. Eric Palmer

Devon County Councillors (March 1989), with their Chairman, Mr Arnold Sayers

A nostalgic scene – one of the County Council's steamrollers and road gang pictured at Staverton in 1905

Historic opening by the Minister of Transport, Dr Leslie Burgin, of the Exeter By-pass in February 1938 (Western Morning News)

Work in progress in 1972 on the new A38 dual carriageway road south west of Exeter at Haldon Hill

suburban parts of the County also gained seats in 1955 and 1961. The result was that the number of councillors rose from 78 in 1889 to 91 in 1961.

Reorganisation in 1973 demanded a new pattern of electoral areas to accommodate the inclusion of the former county boroughs, and as each division had to be on average much larger, a new system was created quickly by the application of very crude rules. A more sophisticated operation was undertaken in order to redraw areas for the 1985 elections, and the Council, which had been 98 in 1973, was reduced to 85 as a result of this.

Electoral behaviour

Some aspects of electoral behaviour made an obvious contribution to the working of the member-recruitment system whilst others have no connection with the work of the Council itself.

Turnout is an example of the latter. Though of great interest in its own right it does not affect decision-making directly or indirectly. In the first elections voter participation in general was very high by later standards of English local government elections, and many of the contests were very close. There were also a few 'hopeless' candidatures which were reflected in a very low vote for the loser. The first elections established a tradition of public meetings both to sort out candidatures without a public election and to demonstrate and mobilise support for one person. When candidates did not hold meetings, or individuals tried to pre-empt the process, this was a matter for adverse comment. The impression given from press reports is of intense political activity when a contest took place but widespread satisfaction or acquiescence when it did not. Where a division was contested turnout ranged from 80 to over 90 per cent.

Statistics for turnout in ordinary or bye-elections between 1892 and 1937 are not generally available but the evidence of figures sporadically quoted from time to time suggests a slow decline, particularly in the interwar years, and reports of election meetings become fewer. Between 1946 and 1970 the decline continued and published statistics show the following situation:

	1946	1949	1952	1955	1958	1961	1964	1967	1970
% voting in contests	41.8	45.6	39.2	33.6	30.0	31.0	25.8	37.1	27.3

In the first elections for the new system turnout leapt to 50% and it has remained at a much higher level than in the 1950s and 1960s – in 1985 it was 44.5%. The difference is more impressive when it is noted that the post-reorganisation figures are for all divisions rather than for only the fifth or quarter of them that were contested. However, except for the first elections, each year has involved great variation between divisions. As examples, in 1961 turnouts included Teignmouth East (9.5%), Axminster (16.5%), Great Torrington (46.2%) and Buckfastleigh (47.8%). The picture for 1985 shows a much more homogeneous pattern but there was still variation from Wellswood (33.8%) to Trelawney (60.3%).

58

Competitiveness was a much more significant factor for the Council as an organisation because it affected the stability of membership over time. Between 1892 and 1970 the proportion of seats contested varied from year to year for no obvious reasons, but each major period had its characteristic level of competitiveness. The new system was completely different from the start: the multi-party system guaranteed that all seats would be contested, usually by more than two candidates.

The inevitable degree of uncertainty about 'clean sweep' elections tends to produce more candidates and this was the case with the 1889 elections. The number of contested divisions – 26 out of 78 seats, and 5 out of 10 by-elections in February, 1889 – was greater than at any election until 1946. Once the original membership had been established the system settled down to a relatively small number of contests each third year, though there was an unexplained cyclical variation before the First World War: 26 – 10 – 6 – 12 – 5 – 11 – 6 – 15 – 5 [actual numbers not vouched for]. There were very rarely more than two candidates, though press reports indicated that before nominations closed three or more were considering standing. A similar variation was observed in the interwar period: 6 – 13 – 12 – 8 – 11 – 15 [again actual numbers not vouched for] but with a few more multi-member contests.

From 1946 to 1970 the aggregate figures are available in official publications: 41 – 26 – 19 – 20 – 19 – 20 – 32 – 21 – 15 [the latter number is for 75 divisions only as opposed to 83–91 for the previous elections]. The number of contests involving more than 2 candidates remained very low, 4.7% of total divisions and 17% of contested divisions.

By-elections and ordinary elections

A special note must be made of by-elections because these played a much more important role in the County Council than they have done in national politics. Bye-elections were suspended during the two world wars and replaced by co-option but otherwise mid-term vacancies were filled in the conventional manner. As members tended to serve for as long as they possibly could those involved in the system thought of 'vacancies' as occurring when an incumbent died, resigned in mid-term, or announced that he (or she) was not seeking re-election.

By-elections for councillor seats were also created by the aldermanic system. 'Vacancies' on the aldermanic bench occurred through serving members dying, resigning and not seeking re-election. Then, when a councillor was 'promoted', another by-election was caused. In 1889 ten councillors were elected aldermen and this led to ten by-elections in early February. This set a pattern for the future; every third year there was the likelihood of one or more of such vacancies consequent upon the ordinary aldermanic elections.

The impact of this factor in the traditional system may be summarised as follows: approximately 115 new members entered as a result of by-elections caused by the aldermanic system, 127 through peacetime by-elections caused by councillors ceasing to be members, and 53 through wartime co-option.

To these sources of change in membership should be added the turnover at ordinary elections caused by incumbents not seeking re-election and being defeated. Before 1973 in many parts of the County the triennial elections were treated like by-elections in that only if the serving member made it clear that he or she was not seeking re-election did other candidates come forward. Defeat in an ordinary election was a relatively rare cause of departure from the Council though some 'resignations' were probably anticipations of defeat or a sign of unwillingness to bear the costs of electioneering. However, if incumbents fought an opposed election they were normally successful. The aggregate effect was that generally between 15% and 25% of the Council were 'freshmen' immediately after each ordinary election.

After reorganisation the political situation changed and so did the role of bye-elections and incumbency. Between 1973 and 1977 control of the Council depended on the Conservatives not losing four by-elections; between 1985 and 1989 they or the Alliance could have gained an absolute majority by winning six or seven by-elections. In these circumstances there is pressure on individuals not to resign in mid-term. At ordinary elections incumbency ceased to be the great protection that it was under the non-partisan system and national swings in party popularity produced unprecedented changes in local Council membership. The result is that the new system has worked very differently. In 1977 over 40% of the Council had not been members in 1973; in 1981 over 50% were new and about 50% in 1985 had carried through from 1981, though this was partly a consequence of the reduction in the number of seats.

The aldermanic system, 1889–1974

County councils before reorganisation had to contain an indirectly elected element. The first business of the provisional council in January, 1889, was to elect a temporary chairman and a number of aldermen equal to one third of number of councillors, in the case of Devon 26. A half of these had to retire after three years and the other half after six (1892 and 1895 respectively) but after those dates each 'cohort' served for six years. Individuals could seek re-election indefinitely, and need not have been councillors before first being elected an alderman. Only councillors could vote in aldermanic elections but the chairman had a casting vote in the event of a tie. Ordinary aldermanic elections were suspended during the two wars, though by-elections continued.

The provisional Devon County Council at its first meeting had great difficulty establishing how aldermanic elections should be conducted and the councillors eventually voted for 128 individuals, of which 37 received only one vote and another 51 between two and nine votes. The most popular candidate – Sir John Phear – received 60 votes and the 4 least popular of those elected 20

	elected	defeated	total	% successful
'outsiders'	16	61	77	20.8%
councillors	10	41	51	19.6%
total	26	102	128	20.3%
% outsiders	61.5%	59.8%	60.2%	

votes. 16 of the successful candidates were not councillors, including 2 who had been defeated in the first elections. Some of the non-members who failed to get elected later became councillors and eventually aldermen.

The number of aldermanic seats changed as the number of councillors decreased and increased from time to time, as a result of boundary changes and redistributions of electoral divisions. It started at 26, dropped to 25, rose slowly to 30 in 1961 and then fell to 25 after the changes of 1966–68.

The aldermanic system of Devon County Council deserves special study in its own right, but here only the highlights can be mentioned. Though indirect election was always to some extent controversial at national level and occasionally caused difficulties in Devon, once it had settled down it did in fact become a central feature of the working system of the County Council.

There were 25 ordinary elections, including the first, and one special election in 1968 to accommodate the reduction in membership caused by the boundary changes. The convention was very quickly established that incumbents who wished to continue should be re-elected; only in the very early years and in 1968 was this 'rule' broken. It took a longer period – twenty years – to establish that only councillors could become aldermen. During the same period the principle that the aldermanic bench represented 'promotion' for long-serving members was gradually established, but as everyone was aware of the demands for geographical representation 'years of councillor-ship' was not a rigid determinant of aldermanic electoral outcomes. There is little evidence that partisanship was important but the council did recognise exceptional ability (defined in systemic terms) and a few individuals received relatively rapid advancement to the bench.

The aldermanic system made a considerable contribution to the working of the council and committee system. It protected leading members from changing electoral fortunes – which might bear no relation to the work of the County Council itself – and provided a reliable source of committee chairmen. It decisively tilted the balance of power in favour of the County against sectional interests and the 'backwoodsmen'. Thus, for example, in 1962 aldermen made a disproportionate contribution to the formal leadership of the Council.

	chairmanships	vice-chairmanships	total members
councillors	7	10	91
aldermen	15	11	30

The establishment and stabilisation of the Council's membership

Approximately 275 (not more than 280) individuals served on Devon County Council from 1889 to 1914. Others considered seeking election or actually did so but were not successful; I have counted 201 but that is almost certainly an underestimate. The 'unsuccessful' category includes at least 77 people who were mentioned as possible candidates during 1888 and early 1889, at least 19 possibles between 1892 and 1913 inclusive, at least 55 defeated individuals who did not succeed on another occasion, 33 'outsiders' who were not elected at the first ballot for aldermen, and 15 non-councillors who were supported but not elected as aldermen between 1890 and 1914.

The membership of the council for most of this period was 104 (103 for the rest of the time), of which 78 were councillors and 26 aldermen. The twenty-five years of this period were divided into eight and a third local 'legislatures' by the system of triennial ordinary elections, superimposed upon which were the ordinary aldermanic elections at which a half of the bench was renewed every third year. Both the councillor and the aldermanic election systems provided for by-elections in the normal way; I estimate that there were over 50 by-elections for councillor seats and 20 for the aldermanic bench.

Most of the details of the mechanisms at work in the electoral process and on the Council have been lost for ever, but their consequences for the stability of membership on the County Council are available for everyone to discover. The County Council during this period was dominated by long-serving members. Of those recruited during the period over 50% served for ten years or more, overwhelmingly in continuous tenure, 25% served for over 17 years, and nearly 10% for more than 30 years. Of course for many of them membership continued after 1914 into the interwar years and in a few cases into the post-1945 period. The figures underestimate the involvement of the total membership in county government because many of the first members had already served for a substantial time in Quarter Sessions before 1889. The calculation of their full tenure is truncated by the radical change from appointment to election, which sets the counter back to zero.

This system continued after the First World War. County council elections in Devon had a very clear starting point – the decision of the retiring member whether to seek re-election or not. Between elections this had a counterpart in the decision whether to resign or not, and was supplemented by death and disqualification. A consequence of this is that by-elections took on the character of ordinary elections, or the reverse, depending on which way the processes are conceived. Incumbents dominated ordinary elections, and death, ill-health and 'tiredness' were more important than electoral defeat as sources of the secular change of membership that is necessary for the long-term stability and continuity of the system.

After the Second World War, though there was a rise in competitiveness, incumbents still continued to dominate the electoral process. Each ordinary election produced its 'quota' of long-service members who would eventually take the place of those from Edwardian and 'Georgian' times who led the Council in 1946. The development of the system was complicated by local

aggregate effects on membership stability															
	1892	1895	1898	1901	1904	1907	1910	1913	1916	1919	1922	1925	1928	1931	1934	1937
changes	30	16	20	14	20	27	24	12	*18	*18	33	21	17	20	20	22
total	104	104	104	103	103	103	104	104	100	100	100	102	102	102	102	112

	1940	1943	1946	1949	1952	1955	1958	1961	1964	1967	1970	1970+
changes	*27	*27	*27	35	31	33	28	25	36	32	32	8
total	112	112	112	112	110	118	121	121	118	100	100	100

* = adjusted for the different time spans: 35/2 for 1913–19, 82/3 for 1937–46

government reorganisation. The Council lost some probable veterans through the extension of Exeter and Plymouth and the creation of Torbay in the 1966–68 period and sixty-eight members (of more than 3 years service) had their service terminated by the abolition of the old Devon County Council in 1974. Only a proportion of the serving members in the third period tried to continue into the new systems and not all were successful.

Parties and Partisanship

Younger readers who have been brought up in an environment in which the County Council is a strongly partisan authority may think that too little space has been devoted to political parties. But in the perspective of a hundred years the present system of party organisation of members is a late-comer to the system. Until 1973 'partisanship' at the County level in Devon did not mean what it meant and still means on the urban county councils and the large city councils; the organisation of party members into a 'caucus' with a leader, secretary, whips, standing orders and party meetings prior to council and committee meetings. The basic point is that before 1973 the national party affiliations of most prominent individuals were well known to others and to the electors but that this knowledge entered into county politics in a number of ways.

The greatest degree of complexity was experienced in the period 1889–1919. During this time there were, first, straight Liberal-Conservative (or Unionist) election contests on some occasions and in a few divisions. Everyone knew what was going on and the campaign was organised through the party machinery. Secondly, there was bi-partisanship where an individual candidate received open support, for instance, on the nomination papers, from prominent members of both parties. Thirdly, transpartisanship occurred where an individual, though known to be a member of one party, received widespread support for reasons that cut across party lines. Fourthly, non-partisanship occurred when an individual had no known connection with either party and perhaps had openly rejected any link. A fifth situation, which appears to combine the third and fourth condition, occurred when two known members of the same party were opponents in an election. There is evidence, in the reported speeches and proposals of different individual candidates, of different basic political attitudes within broad party categories: reactionary conservatism, Tory paternalism, Gladstonian liberalism, radicalism, and Liberal Unionism.

All these dimensions of partisanship played a part in the electoral politics of Devon County Council up to and including 1913. Devon local politics did not comprise a one-party Conservative political system. In fact Liberals, and Liberal Unionists before they started to lose their independent existence, played leading roles on the Council. Lord Fortescue, speaking at the annual meeting in March, 1907, remarked that 'for thirteen years it had been their rule and custom that once they were in the Council Chamber politics were left behind and their only object was to do the best they could for the county' (hear, hear). He was probably referring indirectly to the problems of Cornwall

County Council with a Liberal revolt against Conservative monopoly of leading positions within the authority. There may have been a role for partisanship on the Council but if so it operated in a muted and sophisticated way.

In many parts of the country the rise of the Labour Party after 1918 had a considerable affect on the relations between Liberals and Conservatives in local government, forcing them into a local government alliance sometimes called the 'Citizens' Party' or 'Ratepayers Association'. This was not a factor in Devon County elections. In the interwar period the Labour Party was almost completely absent from local politics, except in Plymouth and Exeter, and therefore the pressure for a Liberal-Conservative alliance was lacking. Between 1919 and 1937, therefore, the partisan patterns of the Victorian and Edwardian eras continued, with a reduction in the extent of straightforward party opposition and an increase in members who were not prominent as party activists. But once members were elected their origins tended to be forgotten and they were assessed in terms of their value to the County Council.

In the County Council elections of 1946 the Labour Party made a relatively big effort and won eight seats. After 1946 a reaction seems to have set in and Labour members either did not seek re-election or were defeated. Those that survived the 1949 ordinary elections drifted into de facto independence. As the Party ceased to nominate new candidates except in a very small number of divisions, its representation was in effect non-existent.

After 1945, though pre-war Liberals continued to hold their seats, the recruitment of members of the party formally ceased. A number of independents were well-known as Liberals in national politics but this did not seem to be highly relevant to the electors. However, Devon was in the forefront of the Liberal revival in Parliamentary politics and in the 1960s the Party began to take a greater interest in the County Council. The local authority went out of existence before the strength of this trend could be fully tested.

Before reorganisation, therefore, *party* was an element in the County Council's work but it was not an organised one and did not involve separate steps in the Council's processes. In fact it was normally ignored, for instance, when the actions of central government, whatever its partisan nature, adversely affected Devon's financial position. Members of all parties and independents united to criticise both Conservative and Labour cabinets for inconsistent policies and 'unfair' grant systems. Reorganisation has changed this to a considerable extent but elements of trans-party hostility to the centre can still be detected in the work of the County Council.

The new non-metropolitan or 'shire' county combined the old county boroughs and administrative county. From the 1973 elections onwards Devon experienced party government in the full sense of the phrase. The partisanship of the urban areas was deliberately exported to the rest of the County, partly through pressure put on 'independents' to declare their national allegiance, and partly as a result of the policy of the then-major parties of contesting every division, however unpromising prospects for success were. Liberals were not so uniform in their approach and some independents successfully defied party organisation. Therefore, since reorganisation the internal organisation of the Council has contained another element – the machinery of party 'government'. Council members are now further differentiated in terms of their relationship to the 'leadership' of the authority. All officers, but particularly heads of departments, have had to come to terms with the insertion of extra stages in the decision-making process.

As the Conservatives had an absolute majority for the first three 'legislatures' [1973–77, 1977–81, 1981–85] their attitude could have been decisive by itself. But all three parties did in fact create a very similar form of organisation, with leader and party whip as the central roles. Decision-making since that time has involved party meetings and party leadership action as well as committee deliberations and the work of officers.

The situation changed dramatically in 1985 when the Conservatives lost their overall majority and were replaced by an Alliance administration with a degree of support from the Labour Group on the Council. Another stage was then added to the decision-making process – the informal discussions between the leaders of the two groups. After two years, however, this system broke down when Labour withdrew its support for the Alliance over a crucial issue. The leaders of the Alliance felt unable to continue in these circumstances and since that time the Council has 'muddled through' by means of a series of temporary expedients and interactions between the four party leaderships.

Within the space of less than twenty years, therefore, the County Council has experienced four different types of partisan involvement in decision-making: the traditional non-partisan system (1969–73), single party majority rule (1973–85) and two versions of multi-partism (1985–89). If nothing else the frequency of the changes differentiates the present era from the periods up to 1960 when continuity was the hallmark of the contribution of elected members to the work of the authority and subtlety the characteristic of partisanship.

The previous pages have presented a picture of a membership that exhibited characteristic combinations of continuity and change. This membership had four main tasks: to decide how to administer its powers and duties, to fill the positions created by the system of committees, sub-committees and related bodies, to create a structure of departments and other 'bureaucratic' agencies and to appoint the officers and other employees to staff them.

In the generalisations that follow most of the details have been submerged. The reader should realise, however, that each committee has its own history, with a distinctive pattern of membership and internal decision-making processes, that each department is also an individual organisation in its own right, with its own structure and patterns of behaviour, and that the County Council's own organisation 'reaches out' to its environment and to other bodies in the area and beyond, even to the institutions of the European Community. The main focus here is on the forces and developments that are common to all these dimensions of internal organisation.

Indirect and Direct Administration

The County Council in 1889 faced a major choice between direct and indirect exercise of its powers and duties. The option has always been open in principle to all local authorities to employ other bodies, both public and private, or individuals to undertake the implementation of its policies and broad decisions. This was a favoured administrative device in the early years with the delegation of functions to the justices of the peace, and continued with the use of the police force for many inspection roles. The inspectorate under the *Contagious Diseases (Animals) Acts* were high-ranking policemen in the Devon Constabulary. This device was followed in the interwar years for inspectorates under *Diseases of Animals Acts, Shop Acts, Food & Drugs Acts, Explosives Acts* and *Margarine Act*. Private veterinary surgeons were used to discharge some duties under the Diseases of Animals Acts. By 1926 a panel of 24 veterinary surgeons located throughout the County had been appointed.

The first County Treasurer was William Cotton, the Manager of the National Provincial Bank but on his retirement the Bank itself became the legal Treasurer. This arrangement lasted until after the Second World War when the County's own chief financial officer took over the duties and all financial administration became 'in-house'.

I have not been able to determine the exact position of Coroners and their deputies who were appointed for districts based on Barnstaple, Crediton, Honiton, Okehampton, Stoke Damerel, East Stonehouse and Totnes. Nor am I clear about the administrative status of the County Analyst who for over 60 years was listed as a principal officer (in the 1950s this practice was stopped). The first County Analyst – Alexander W. Blyth – had a London address as had the District Analyst appointed under *Fertilisers & Feeding Stuffs Act, 1893.* But by 1910 the Agricultural Analyst was resident in Exeter. It was not until Thomas Tickle took over in the early 1920s that the County Analyst had an Exeter address.

A good example of indirect administration is to be found in the development of non-elementary education before 1902. In the 1890s the County Council provided 'technical instruction' through scholarships, grants and the commissioning of lecture series. Its own employees were few and carried out prior planning and inspections of recipient institutions. In the twentieth century it has become a direct provider through its own schools, colleges and employees.

Direct administration increased with the passage of time and as will be seen below the 1940s were a period of major change. However the issue of indirect administration has arisen again because of the effect of the 'privatisation' legislation of the 1980s on the local authority as a service-providing agency. Some academic observers have seen local authorities as in general moving away from their direct executive role, as apparently confirmed in the 1940s, towards becoming 'holding companies' or 'indirect administrators', in fact reverting to the late nineteenth century system whereby county councils carried out many of their duties through other bodies.

Delegation to districts and field administration

Delegation to lower-tier authorities is an alternative in many services to the creation of field offices or the use of quangos and private bodies. The early County Council had a preference for the former wherever possible and it played a big part in the early years but as time passed the situation became complicated by the creation of 'claiming' rights in respect of specific services or parts of a service for defined categories of district. The maintenance of main roads was a good example of extensive delegation whilst the *Midwives Act, 1902*, illustrated the problems when some districts refused to accept duties and the County Council had to employ the Medical Officers of Health directly to implement the statute.

Field administration was on a county 'regional' basis for the employment of inspectors of weights & measures, with six areas based on Exeter, Barnstaple, Crediton, Tavistock, Totnes, and Newton Abbot. The County Surveyors were also deployed in a 'regional' scheme, first based on a north-south division and then on Exeter, Totnes and Barnstaple. By 1902 a functional element had been added with the senior County Surveyor being responsible for county buildings and two others in charge of main roads in the two divisions into which the County was divided. Later the surveyor for buildings became the County Architect, and by 1914 the number of highway regions was back to three. By the 1920s architecture had been differentiated into responsibilities for the work of the Mental Hospital & Standing Joint committees and for the Education, Public Health and Mental Deficiency committees, whilst main roads continued on a three-region basis.

The situation in the late 1950s was reported in the evidence to the Local Government Commission for England. This showed that the Health, Weights & Measures, Architects', Fire Services, Welfare and Library organisations worked through operating areas, the number, boundaries and area offices of which differed from service to service. In Planning, Children's and Education the divisions had area committees attached to them and there was delegation of various types in Planning, Highways and Civil Defence. Health was the most complex, with 11 main areas whose 'headquarters' supervised a number of more local arrangements for ambulances, chiropody, health centres, clinics, nurses and midwives, health visitors, home help services, occupational therapy and psychiatric social work.

This choice between delegation and field administration became a major political matter in 1973. The 1972 Act permitted county councils to enter into agency arrangements with its districts for the provision of services and the former county boroughs were very keen that this should be the policy of the new Devon. Eventually, however, the County Council rejected delegation and opted for an elaborate system of area administration with which districts could be associated through area sub-committees.

The Committee System

From the very start the work of the elected members has been dominated by the committee system. It should be noted, however, that a committee system in local government is not just a list of main service and functional committees but includes special as well as standing committees, subcommittees, management committees and boards of governors, area committees, joint committees, working parties and visiting committees. As the headquarters standing committee provides a central focus for most of the other types it will be given most attention.

The committee system evolved gradually over the years. The County Council inherited the practice of having standing committees for enduring responsibilities and creating special committees to deal with special problems that were thought to be short-lived. Every addition of a public duty had to be accommodated within the standing committee system. In the case of minor and very specific duties this could be done by giving them to existing committees but major additions usually obtained a committee of their own. There were occasional mergers of committees but as special committees tended to become permanent the number of standing committees gradually increased over the years. It should be noted, however, that what was counted as a full committee, as opposed to a 'subcommittee', and indeed when a 'special' became a 'standing' committee, was not always clear at the time. The numbers given below must be regarded as approximate but the relative general orders of magnitude are correct.

One generalisation may be made about the frequency of meeting of all types of County Council committees. Bodies tended to meet in the same cycle as the full Council unless there was a good reason for more or less frequent meetings. For instance, in 1960–61 18 committees met quarterly, one five times, two eight times, the Education Committee 11 times, and Plympton Redevelopment 'as needed'.

Number and types of committee

In 1889 the County Council established six standing committees and this number increased in net terms to eight by 1905. Further additions took place before the First World War so that in 1914 there were eleven. After the war there was a steady expansion so that by 1937 the Council had 23 standing committees. The late 1930s and Second World War saw a reduction in numbers to 19 and then 15. By the early 1950s expansion had started again and at the end of the decade the number was back to the twenty-plus of the 1930s. Between 1959 and reorganisation there was little change in total but this concealed a decline in service and an increase in functional committees.

Reorganisation led to a rationalisation of the committee system into a smaller number of major committees, with important sub-committees as thought desirable. The eight standing committees seem to have become a fixed feature but there has been some change at the level of sub-committees.

1889 [6] Finance; County Rate; Visitors of the Lunatic Asylum; Bridges, Main Road & County Buildings; Contagious Diseases (Animals); General Purposes & Parliamentary

1905 [8] Bridges & Main Roads; County Rate; Executive (Diseases of Animals Acts) & Weights & Measures; Finance; General Purposes; Lunatic Asylum; Dartmoor; Education

1914 [11] Agricultural; Bridges, Main Roads & County Buildings; County Rate; Executive (Diseases of Animals Acts) & Weights & Measures; Finance;

General Purposes [including Smallholdings]; Local Taxation; Lunatic Asylum [including Mental Deficiency]; Public Health & Housing; Dartmoor; Education

1925 [15] Agricultural; Bridges, Main Roads & County Buildings; County Rate; Finance; General Purposes [including Weights & Measures]; Local Taxation Licences; Mental Hospital Visiting; Care of the Mentally Defective; Public Health & Housing; Dartmoor Forest Preservation; Education; Maternity & Child Welfare; Welfare of the Blind; Smallholdings (Subcommittee); Diseases of Animals (Subcommittee)

1939 [18] Agricultural; County Roads; County Valuation; Finance; General Purposes [including Weights & Measures]; Local Taxation Licences; Mental Hospital Visiting; Care of the Mentally Defective; Public Health & Housing; Education; Maternity & Child Welfare; Welfare of the Blind; Smallholdings & Allotments (Subcommittee); Diseases of Animals (Subcommittee); Public Assistance; Town & Country Planning; Air Raid Precautions; Parliamentary

1953 [19+2] Chairmen & Special Purposes; Children's; Civil Defence; Coast Protection (special); Dartmoor National Park; Diseases of Animals; Education; Establishment; Finance; Fire Brigade; Health; Joint Staff; Legal & General Purposes; Local Taxation Licences; North Devon Floods (special); Planning; Roads; Smallholdings; Supplies; Water & Housing; Welfare

1970 [22] Chairmen & Vice-Chairmen of Committees; Chairmen & Special Purposes; Children's; Dartmoor National Park; Education; Emergency; Estates; Exmoor National Park; Finance; Health; Joint Staff; Legal & General Purposes; Libraries & Museums; Management Services; Planning; Redevelopment; Road Safety & Traffic; Roads; Smallholdings; Social Services; Supplies; Welfare

1987 [8] Policy [Finance, Property & Performance Review, Personnel, Procedures, Energy]; Amenities & Countryside [no subcommittees]; Dartmoor National Park [Commons]; Economy & Employment [Smallholdings]; Education [Community Education, County Awards, Further, Nominations, Resources, Schools, Teachers, Staff]; Planning & Transportation [Planning, Road Safety, Transport Co-ordination]; Public Protection [none]; Social Services [none]

What is strikingly different today is the systematic organisation of area committees and subcommittees. Such arrangements had always been a part of county government but 1973 saw the dimension made into a principle of organisation.

For council members the internal organisational system was completed by the management committees for institutions, visiting committees, working parties and special committees established to investigate specific problems. In addition there were joint arrangements to which the County Council contributed members of the governing body. The best known was the

Standing Joint Committee which controlled the police from 1889 until the 1960s and which consisted of thirteen members nominated by Devon and thirteen by Quarter Sessions. The County Council now nominates twenty members of its successor – the Devon and Cornwall Police Authority. Consultative relations with county districts and the National Health Service also bring into existence a number of committees, but these are not executive bodies.

Co-option to committees and subcommittees

Over the decades delegation has become less important as a means of involving areas and interests in direct administration of county council services, and the co-option of individuals as representatives and experts to the relevant committees and subcommittees has grown. The co-option may take the form of selection by the County Council or nomination by the outside body.

The key event was the establishment of the Education Committee under the 1902 Act. The latter required local education authorities to devise a scheme for the composition of the committee which included individuals with experience of education and acquaintance with the needs of different types of schools. Devon's scheme created a membership of 48 – 32 council members and 16 others, including at least 3 but not more than 5 women, and representatives from the teaching unions, secondary, technical, commercial and industrial education, and both council and voluntary elementary schools. Appointments were to be for three years rather than the one year that was general for other committees. Communications were received about representation from the teaching unions and the churches.

This format has become more common with the passage of time. In 1929 co-opted or nominated members were to be found on the Education, County Valuation, Public Health and Housing, Care of the Mentally Defective, Maternity and Child Welfare, Agriculture, and Welfare of the Blind committees. In 1960 committees whose membership included 'outsiders' were Children's, Civil Defence, Dartmoor National Park, Diseases of Animals, Education, Exmoor National Park, Fire Brigade, Health, Joint Staff Committee, Planning, Smallholdings, Water and Sanitation, and Welfare. By 1987 as the following list shows, co-option was most noticeable at the level of sub-committees: Dartmoor National Park and its Commons Subcommittee, Smallholdings Subcommittee, Education and most of its subcomittees, Road Safety Subcommittee, County/Districts Joint Consultative Committee, County/Health Joint Consultative Committee and District Health joint consultative committees, and all the area committees and subcommittees for education, highways, social services, and Northam Burrows Advisory Committee.

Nominations to other bodies

The converse of co-option from the outside is nomination to other public and private organisations. This has always been a noticeable feature of the work of County Council members. At the start the main outside agencies involving

County Council members were the Standing Joint Committee (13) and the Devon Sea Fisheries Committee (10) and the Boards of Conservators for Fishery Districts (but many of the latter nominations were not members). When Devon decided to join the County Councils' Association it had to provide three delegates. It was perhaps fortunate in that for the latter it had a choice of Parliamentarians from both Houses.

By 1904 little had changed in this respect but by 1929 the University College of the South West (1) and Seale Hayne College (3), three area assessment committees [36] the Voluntary Hospitals Committee (2) showed a tendency for the practice of nomination to increase.

By 1960 there were too many to list. There were 4 County Councils' Association, 13 Standing Joint Committee and 10 Devon Sea Fisheries Committee but in addition there were 39 places in water administration, at least 19 in higher education, 27 for bodies associated with central government's field administration, 7 for bodies associated with the National Health Service, 8 for regional 'Whitley' machinery, a considerable number for local valuation panels (but not all nominees were County Council members), and a handful for other public or private bodies.

In 1987 the Association of County Councils asked for not only 4 Executive Committee members but also 8 members for its standing committees and also officer advisors. The Devon and Cornwall Police Authority required 20 nominations but the Devon Sea Fisheries Committee had dropped to 9. Organisations in the fields of the arts, sport, recreation, tourism, conservation and history provided 28 places to be filled. There were 15 nominations in water administration, the National Health Service demanded 16 nominations, other public bodies 10, and the University 16. There were also 8 other places to be filled by the Council. In addition there were 135 nominations to be made by committees but not all of these were County Council members.

The Departmental System

The departmental system dominates the working lives of employees. A typical local authority department should be seen as consisting of headquarters staff, area offices, satellites in the form of institutions and depots, and close associates in the quasi-private sector – in effect local 'quangos'. Each department is also likely to have close associates in the rest of the public sector.

Not until 1963 were the headquarters of departments gathered together in one main building – the purpose built County Hall on Topsham Road, Exeter. In the early years the Castle and and neighbouring Bradninch Hall were the focus of staff employment but by the early 1960s departments were scattered all over central Exeter and in some cases located in the suburbs. In addition to the traditional buildings there were headquarters offices in St David's Hill, Coaver, Middlemoor, Okehampton Road, Queen Street, Larkbeare, Heavitree Road, Bellair, Clyst St George, Sidwell Street, Whipton, New North Road, and Barley House. With the exception of the 'depot'-based services and functions the departments were largely concentrated in the new building, but it quickly proved to be too small and since then there have been cycles of expansion into other locations and a return to an extended County Hall.

Numbers and size of departments

It is much more difficult to obtain reliable and detailed evidence for the departmental system and the number of staff employed than it is for the committee system and elected representatives. The existence of other work-locations in addition to headquarters confuses the statistics because some sources include officials in institutions and depots and others do not.

It is, however, clear that in 1889 the number of full-time staff directly employed by the County Council was very small. The Clerk to the Council himself was part-time, the treasurer was a local banker and there was a mere handful of 'clerks' employed on County business. By the late 1930s the larger departments – Finance, Education, Public Health, Architectural, Agricultural, County Roads, Public Assistance – were described as having 'staffs numbering many hundreds in aggregate', whilst the Clerk's Department consisted of the Clerk, his Deputy (who also acted as County Solicitor) and 31 clerks. A group photograph of the County Surveyor's staff in 1928 shows 27 men, but obviously does not include manual workers.

Since then the number and range of staff has undoubtedly increased massively. For the 1980s the number is usually given as over 33,000, but this includes an estimated 16,000 part-time employees. Within these numbers is a great range of professions and occupations including the most and the least highly skilled.

The processes of expansion and consolidation

Two significant developments in the first decade of the twentieth century were the creation of an Education Department after 1902 headed by a Secretary and including its own architect and inspectors, and the appointment of a Medical Officer of Health in 1908. On appointment George Adkins headed a staff of only three inspectors, one nurse, two clerical assistants but no tuberculosis officers, school dentists or welfare workers, but he immediately began to expand the functions and therefore the size of his department. He became Chief School Medical Officer with assistants based on Barnstaple and Plymouth and from 1912 built up the tuberculosis service, maternity, child welfare, and developed a County involvement in housing and related matters.

Expansion took the form of either adding new posts to existing departments or creating new organisations. For instance, in the 1920s the County appointed an Organiser of Agricultural Education and this remained a principal officer post until the service was absorbed by the Education Department after the War. The interwar years added a number of specialisms in the personal health and welfare fields and it was not always easy to see how they fitted into an overall plan of administration.

The postwar period was marked by several developments. First, in the late 1940s there was an increase in the number of departments with the expansion of service responsibilities. By 1949 departments for the Fire Services, Planning, Children's, Libraries and, shortly after, Civil Defence, had been established. Secondly, with the growth in size of departments the importance of the role of deputy chief officer increased and in the leading ones the

72

position was treated as deserving public recognition, particularly the deputies for the Clerk, Treasurer, Medical Officer of Health, Chief Education Officer, and for a short time, Surveyor. Another major development was the combination of all aspects of consumer protection under the 'umbrella' of a trading standards service.

The appointment of a County Supplies Officer in the mid-1950s was the first step in a major organisational development within the County Council – the recognition of the importance of functions which cut across the traditional division of activities into separate services. The 1960s saw the addition of the heads of O&M and Establishments, Information and County Records to the list of senior positions.

Some spheres of activity have proved remarkably difficult to organise in an authoritative and unchallenged manner. Over the decades one of the most difficult has been that which includes the various types of local public works, including roads, bridges, buildings and the planning of the physical environment. The traditional professions of surveying, civil engineering and architecture can claim a major role in decision-making in these spheres as can the new expertise based on geography, economics and sociology. The County Council has changed the relationships between them on several occasions. The same could be said of the personal social services for many decades. But in this case the matter was finally settled by two developments in the early 1970s. First, the creation of a unified Social Services Department under the 1970 Act brought together a diverse set of activities that dealt with disadvantaged individuals of many different types and, incidentally, also created an area organisation which was favourably mentioned by the Bains Committee. Secondly, the reorganisation of the National Health Service in 1973 made the problems of relations between the personal social and health services an inter-organisational matter rather than an internal one.

Other employee organisations

For many citizens the County Council was and is only 'real' because of the existence of satellites in the form of institutions and depots in which specialised staff work, particularly those who deal directly with the public and private groups.

Unfortunately there is no space to do more than mention these. For the first fifty-five years the most important individual institution was the Devon County Asylum, later the Devon Mental Hospital, but this eventually passed into the National Health Service. Colleges and schools were and are quantitatively the most important local institutions – over 560 in 1986. The social services contributed children's and old people's homes, hostels, training centres, sheltered workshops and day care centres. The library service involved, in addition to headquarters, 5 area central, 78 local and 17 mobile libraries. The most important 'depots' were the 58 fire stations and the numerous sites involved in local public works.

Conditions of Employment and Unionisation

The Council began with very few full-time headquarters staff. Their remuneration, conditions of work and pensions were dealt with on an *ad hoc* basis and described and discussed in the Council minutes and meetings. The Council had a larger staff deployed in institutions, depots and area organisation and these were also treated in a public and personal manner.

The creation of the Education Department as a result of the 1902 Act was a significant event. Though education required a large staff located in schools and colleges it also needed a substantial headquarters administration, including inspectors, architects and medical officers. From the first, education was an 'organisation within the organisation' and developed a more systematic approach to qualifications, recruitment, grading and pay.

Until the Second World War there were no national schemes governing local authority employment. The 1930s still exhibited a pattern of collective bargaining that was fragmented, 'random and piecemeal', with great differences between areas in levels of pay and conditions and competition between councils for qualifications in short supply. Some progress had been made in relation to teachers and to manual workers but innovations for 'white collar' staff had been short-lived. The National Joint Council for Administrative, Professional, Technical and Clerical Staff was established at the end of the war and countrywide collective bargaining became the method of settling employment matters for the named types of employees.

Devon County Council had not generally supported developments at national level in the 1920s and there was a substantial number of council members who opposed developments in the superannuation system and in national collective bargaining. These attitudes continued to be strong after 1945 and it took a number of episodes to establish that Devon could not opt out of the national economy and society.

The local branch of NALGO originated as a County Council Staff Association in 1919 but was always in fact part of that union. It developed slowly in the 1920s and 1930s until it enjoyed a quantum leap in 1942 with the creation of local joint machinery in the form of a Joint Staff Committee. Before reorganisation the employers were represented by very senior council members which was a source of strength for the Committee.

Personnel administration

As the Council's full-time staff increased in numbers and complexity there was a growing awareness of the need for machinery at both council member and officer levels to deal with the issues and problems that these developments raised.

At first staffing matters were dealt with by individual departments and the treasurer's department as appropriate and it was not until the 1960s that the establishment function was recognised in the appointment of a specialist with chief officer status. Since that time the function has grown in importance and formal organisation.

A 'Special Staffing Committee' was created in March 1929 to deal with salary or emoluments of County officials and this quickly became known as the Establishment Committee. This remained a standing committee until the late

1960s when it became part of Management Services and was then transmuted into the Personnel Subcommittee of the Policy Committee at reorganisation.

Leadership Within the Organisation

The above descriptions of the internal structure of Devon County Council have treated as separate each of the characteristic organisations created for council members and officers. This leaves out an important factor: members and officers are continually interacting with each other and decision-making rarely if ever involves only one dimension of the Council's operating system. The interactions of members and officers constitute a leadership system for the local authority and the development and working of this is the subject of the final chapter.

5

DEVON'S LEADERSHIP

E very large organisation has formal leaders, that is, individuals who are recognised by others both inside and outside the system as its heads and who occupy roles involving a degree of ceremony and ritual. Formal leaders are often also informal leaders, that is, individuals who help to make things happen, who exercise an influence on what goes on within its boundaries, who represent the organisation in and to the rest of the world – in short, those who make a disproportionate contribution to decision-making.

A few words of apology are owed to all those who have been and are involved in the work of the local authority without receiving any publicity and at lower levels in the system. Because of the social and political prominence that leaders enjoy, their contribution to the system is easily over-estimated. Devon County Council has over the hundred years turned into a large organisation providing a wide range of services and affecting County society, economy and daily life in a multitude of ways. These functions cannot be fulfilled without the contributions of a large body of men and women employed by the Council and more diverse groups of citizens who are associated with the work of the authority. For reasons of space these parts of the working system can only be mentioned in passing in other chapters and not given a chapter to themselves.

Leadership in local authorities

Three general points need to be made about leadership within Devon County Council. These relate to one important function of local leadership which is to provide a degree of political and administrative stability in the working of the local authority.

First, the two spheres in which political stability was most important and most apparent in Devon were *county-district* relations and *central-local* relations. Not responding to the demands of either could cause long-term difficulties for everyone but as *localism* and the centre 'pushed' (and still 'push') county councils in different directions, reacting promptly and favourably to the demands of one could have adverse effects on relations with the other. County councils were responsible for general county policies which were supposed to embody the principles and standards laid down – with varying degrees of insistence – by the central government. As localism had maximum scope for expression in the lower tier, threats to the stability of the system were found in the towns and villages of the County whose interests could gain powerful representation through the electoral process within the County Council itself. From 1889 to 1973 the danger was that the 'backwoodsmen' would provoke serious conflict between the county and the centre. After 1973 the danger was that a localism based on Plymouth, Exeter or Torbay would prevent the County Council developing county-wide perspectives.

Every sphere of decision-making reveals a potential for disruptive conflict between either the centre or the districts and the County Council. All reorganisations of services within the County, particularly those that involved divisional administration, delegation to county districts, co-option to county committees and the location of institutions and depots, were good examples of the problems of county-district relations, whilst reactions to legislation and national policy changes in major services, such as education, were examples of central-local relations. The closing of an individual village school on the ground that it is too small is an example of a county-wide policy often strongly resisted by local people, whilst the creation of divisional executives under the 1944 Act led to serious trouble with the Ministry of Education in 1945.

Some of the problems came up frequently. The making of the county precept each year was an occasion for a confrontation between the 'kings men' and the 'country party', and contrasts with 'one-off' problems such as the building of a new county hall. For the County Council what was important was that those with a county perspective should generally have more power and influence within the organisation than those who thought in local and 'parochial' terms – who tended to give great emphasis to local needs and to demand special treatment even if this meant discounting national policies.

Secondly, a modern local authority needs leadership at both the elected-representative and the departmental levels. When they are combined the result is *political management*, a phrase which reflects the necessity for both a lay and a professional input into the guidance and co-ordination of the whole system. Political leadership can only be provided by elected representatives. Only they have the ultimate legitimacy to stand up to the central government and other public bodies, to force reconciliations on competing interests, and eventually to choose courses of action that favour some groups at the expense of others. Administrative leadership can only be provided by full-time staff with relevant expertise, managerial ability and the powers of control and co-ordination over other employees.

Political management occurs when leading council members and leading officials combine to reinforce each other's work, when elected representatives provide the framework and support for executive leadership and when chief officers facilitate the exercise of political leadership within the authority and towards the outside world. Leadership activities tend to exist in pairs, one half being the contribution of council members and the other being the input of the paid staff. They are thus a consequence of the pattern of organisation as a whole.

Thirdly, either all political systems are social systems or every social system has its political aspects. Leaders are individuals as well as the temporary occupants of roles within the organisational system. For men and women tenure of senior positions interacts with their membership of the society at large. Local political and administrative behaviour, including the actions of local leaders, involves the ordinary processes of organisational recruitment, socialisation and control and many other social activities, such as friendship and the achievement of personal ambitions. Organisational processes are themselves simply examples of the ubiquitous processes of everyday life whereby, for instance, individuals attain, adapt to and modify roles which are the elements of the social system. Both officers and members have calculable 'life chances' within and outside the County Council and pursue a 'career' of which it is only a part.

The development of leadership within Devon County Council

It follows from the above that the evolution of a leadership system within the County Council involved two lines of development, one within the elected membership and one within the employees, and each of these required people as individuals and organisational 'devices' through which they could work. In this respect the changes in Devon County Council's management were identical with the 'institutionalisation' exhibited, since the end of the First World War, by the Soviet Politburo, the American Presidency, and the British Cabinet. Devon County Council was a complex organisation and became more so during the period of study. Its officer-structure developed towards greater elaboration and there was an increasing tendency to make use of modern management techniques. The committee system settled down into a regular structured pattern. Relations with outside bodies were also system-atised by formal agreements covering exchange of members through co-option and nomination arrangements. Without the payment of salaries to council members it is impossible to develop much further than has been achieved since 1973 in the direction of a 'professional' legislative system.

In simplest terms the system required a loyalty from individuals to the County Council rather than to districts and professions. Devon needed support for county-wide objectives, the willingness of individuals to do more than the legal minimum in pursuit of the County interests, and the capacity of a few to undertake leadership roles. It needed to develop a system of 'horizontal' committees and departments to offset the parochialism of politics and the excessive professionalism of service specialists. Everyone who has studied local government recognises that the commitment of council members and officers to progress in each service separately has been a major factor in the development of local government but also it is widely recognised that the conventional system contains the twin dangers of 'committee-itis' and 'departmentalism'.

Political Leadership

The study of political leadership within a local authority must begin before individuals are even nominated as candidates. As elected representatives come from and remain members of local society the process of acquiring favourable attitudes towards the County Council – *pre-socialisation* – is vital to the long-term political stability of the system. The 'products' of pre-socialisation are then taken over by the 'mechanisms' of the electoral process and the result is a council membership from which the political leaders must be drawn. The next process is *socialisation* within the local authority itself and this leads on to the 'promotion' system within the membership.

The social bases of council membership

The characteristics of the people who achieve public office are important factors in understanding the decision-making behaviour of public authorities. One of the most important issues debated when the creation of county councils was discussed in the nineteenth century was whether the principle of direct election would work at the level of the county itself. Public bodies can always find paid officers by offering the right salary and 'fringe' benefits, but the recruitment of elected representatives depends on the moral and political attitudes of individuals within the electorate at large. The recoupment of expenses incurred by local council membership has only been possible since 1948; the system was expanded at reorganisation and has been modified since then, but its function still remains one of enabling individuals to participate rather than of rewarding them for their contribution.

Research into local political leadership lies half-way between the study of mass behaviour, where the individual can be completely ignored, and the study of the Prime Minister or President, where the individual is everything. At the electoral level, in a county such as Devon, a few individuals, sometimes one alone, could make a considerable difference to the overt and measurable aspects of local political behaviour, especially in the traditional non-partisan system. An electoral division could be contested simply because there was one person who ignored the influence of incumbency or was a 'persistent defeatist', or a rural ward could be partisan because a village contained one fervent and active member of the Labour Party. At the level of the County Council at any given time only one local 'chancellor of the exchequer' was needed to chair the Finance Committee and only one person could be chairman of the Council itself.

When the first complex systems of local government were being consciously created, in the last twenty years of the nineteenth century, it was rightly believed that distinct levels of society could be detected in rural and small-town Britain. The key factor was the ability to travel, which was itself a function of the availability of means of transport and, from the point of view of the individual, income. Thus throughout the county there was a level of society which contained people – landowners in rural areas and capitalists in urban areas – who were able to make the day's journey necessary to serve on a county council ('government by horse and trap'). In the towns service was in principle open to everyone as travel costs were virtually non-existent, and special provisions were introduced to make sure that ordinary people could serve on parish councils, leaving the rural district as an intermediate body, to which the smaller property-owner was suited.

Those who were elected to the first county councils have been described by J. M. Lee as 'social leaders' because they owed their political position to their socio-economic status. As they have tended to disappear completely in the twentieth century the 'theory' of county government was undermined and it was necessary to recruit another sort of person to fill the roles the system prescribed. Lee found the people in 'public persons' – those who obtained a social status from their widespread political and administrative activities.

The early county councils in Devon were undoubtedly of high social status. As has been mentioned already they included peers of the realm, national politicians, large landowners, successful businessmen, leading professionals and the representatives of large categories such as tenant farmers. Many were also active at lower levels in the system and in the machinery of justice. A few were active writers and lecturers in addition to their other roles. In the late twentieth century leaders had built up positions for themselves by their extensive and often devoted public service.

The social and political characteristics of council members

About nine hundred and fifty individuals have served on Devon County Council since its creation in 1889. What sort of people were they and how did the system accommodate to changes in membership over the years? How was a changing society reflected within the County Council itself?

First, the most striking factor is the *individuality* of the political recruitment processes. The membership of Devon County Council during each period has been sufficiently small for the student to regard every candidate, councillor and alderman as an individual, especially as it is possible, by using a variety of historical sources, to find out a considerable amount about their personal characteristics – even down to where they took their holidays and what they said in public speeches.

Secondly, the general features of the social system and of related political conflict moulded the processes through which individuals actually came to be members of the County Council by encouraging or discouraging candidatures and increasing or reducing the ability of individuals to get elected. The two major social factors were *sex* and *age* and there were four main sources of political conflict: *place, class, religion* and *partisanship*.

Individuality and the local political career

Although certain classes, types or categories of person may constitute a disproportionately large percentage of the membership of a council the reverse is invariably not the case. Candidates for council seats are a tiny fraction of any social group. In the 1950s candidates for Devon County Council formed about 0.0328% of the total electorate; farmers and landowners constituted noticeable proportions of the membership of the County Council during most of this period but most farmers were not candidates, councillors or aldermen.

There are four factors that are central to *individuality* in Devon – *family*, specific *occupation and place of work*, *membership* of private organisations and *service* on other bodies – and they have an important characteristic in common: they involve prior socialisation and 'politicisation'. To the first corresponds the *political family*, to the second the *politicised occupation and location*, to the third the *politicised organisation* and to the fourth the *political career*.

The existence of political families is well recognised at the national level in many countries, but little attention has been paid to identical phenomena at local level. In Devon in the early years *family* and *kinship* played a role in socialisation towards and recruitment to the County Council. It is difficult to get reliable and complete evidence on kinship factors but there were numerous examples of sons, daughters, grandsons and wives of serving or former members being elected. At least a dozen of the traditional county families were represented over a period of several decades, in some cases from the date of the first county council election in 1889 through to the 1950s. There was a noticeable number of father-son successions, also brothers and cousins were found serving together, and in later years husband-wife and father-daughter successions. Before 1914 amongst the families contributing more than one member were the Aclands, Amorys, Arnolds, Holleys, Bastards, Wallops, Lopes, Mallocks, Morleys, Moore-Stevens and Edgcumbes. This list is certainly incomplete and underestimates the family connection because some of the 'successions' took place in the interwar years.

But even *family* does not completely explain the activation of individuals. There are some families noticeable for their absence. In particular, the Northcotes and Courtenays, prominent in politics in the third quarter of the nineteenth century, are entirely or largely absent from county government after 1889. Other well-known families contributed only one individual, often serving for only a short time. And within the 'political families' most individuals did not serve on the County Council. Further analysis is required in order to portray the roles of non-traditional families who contributed more than one individual to the membership of the Council, and the motivation of ambitious 'incomers' who have no family background in County affairs.

Individuality in class terms involves the rejection of conventional class or status systems, for instance, those devised by the Registrar General, as seriously misleading. The notion of 'economic class' is something that is superimposed upon an enormous range of specific employments. What matters is the actual occupations of the individuals. For most of the hundred years in Devon the categories of an urban society based on big cities were not appropriate to the traditional rural and small-town social structure. Jobs vary tremendously in the extent to which they are politicised occupations, that is, those whose tenancy exposes the individual to political experiences, thus increasing political knowledge, awareness and often resources. An occupation may either motivate an individual or provide him or her with means and opportunity, including information, to seek election. In extreme cases such as working as a local government officer, the degree of knowledge attained will be very high. In partisan areas the access of different occupations to service on the council is channelled through the party organisation; this tends to act mainly as a filter in one party areas to exclude those who tend to support the other parties. The most common specific occupation was farmer (yeoman, agriculturalist, land agent), followed by the higher ranks of the armed forces, from army major to general. 'Landowner' was also frequently given, though it was sometimes accompanied by other titles. Professions represented included minister of religion, medicine, the law, banking and engineering. Manufacturers were also a noticeable category, but what is probably significant is the actual industry – textiles, drink, paper, ships, boots and shoes, gas. Merchants also came from several different spheres of commerce – iron, clay, drink, books, shipping.

Complications arise under this heading because of the non-specific descriptions sometimes used – 'partner', 'contractor', 'merchant', 'trader', 'company chairman', and worst of all 'gentleman'. The last is sometimes an indication that the individual is retired but it may also indicate a private income of some sort or simply a desire not to identify with something more specific.

Less obviously, specific workplaces and places of resort may contain a politicised atmosphere which will affect all those exposed to it. And certain social and economic organisations are *per se* connected with the world of government and thus politicise in particular their office-holders. There is no space to explore these factors.

The individual local political career

Individuality as represented by the third and fourth factors require the notion of a *local political career* which embraces membership of different public bodies and private organisations. Such memberships are sources of pre-socialisation and are ways of creating a political reputation.

A major factor was the involvement of the individual in other public roles. It is clear that in the early years the recruitment of County Council members often started in the machinery of justice or in membership of district and parish councils or their forerunners. Individuals active in politics often seem to gather to themselves a number of public roles and this factor undoubtedly played a part in the recruitment processes of Devon County Council during this period.

First, a considerable number of those active in Quarter Sessions transferred to the County Council, so that the 'old' outnumbered the 'new' in the early years – 65 against 39. This factor declined in importance for obvious reasons, but it continued in another form. Members of Quarter Sessions were justices of the peace and the connections between the county council and the judicial function remained close. But once county councils were established it is possible for the recruitment process to 'flow' in the other direction: council members were appointed as justices. As the research on this point has not been completed it is only possible to point to the large number of joint memberships; in 1914 24 out of 26 aldermen and 32 out of 77 councillors were justices, 54% of the total.

Secondly, the existence of a large number of lower level elected authorities provided a continuing source of new members. District level service on boards of guardians, local boards and district councils was widely treated as a relevant factor in candidatures. The County Council therefore resembled many other multi-tier systems in which 'promotion' upwards was regarded as a normal political process. In later years this type of progression upwards contributed to the working of the system, which needed to create a set of public persons who are able to fill the roles previously filled by social leaders.

Service on a lower-tier authority was almost always easier for the individual and elections were much more predictable because of the social meaningfulness of the constituencies. A person could therefore begin to establish a reputation for being politically competent and to acquire a taste for local government. Thus when a 'vacancy' occurred because the serving county councillor died, became an alderman, resigned or did not seek re-election, an individual would consider whether to try for 'promotion'. If he or she succeeded and showed an ability in county affairs then he or she created a role for him- or herself which reinforced itself the longer the service on the County Council. Members of district councils were aware of the concept of a 'vacancy' and both acted and spoke in a way that suggests that it was widely accepted as a determinant of recruitment. When new candidates announced their intention they made reference to the fact that the incumbent was not seeking re-election; their behaviour in refraining from standing in ordinary elections, yet contesting a subsequent by-election, was also testimony to their basic attitude.

The contribution of service on a district or parish council can be illustrated by the 1961 elections. Of the 90 candidates for whom evidence is available at least 75% were on district councils, others were parish councillors and some were both. The impression given today is that service on two levels at the same time is more difficult and only about 25% of the County Council are also district councillors. The volatility of party fortunes also makes the pursuit of a multi-level 'career' more difficult than it was under nonpartisanship, and the system must be regarded as not yet fully established in this respect.

Thirdly, in addition to the machinery of justice and district authorities, there were many representational roles in economic and social organisations and these were often regarded as important qualifications for elevation to the County Council. Unfortunately it is impossible to do justice to this factor here.

Age and sex

In the anthropological tradition the roles of women and the aged in the political process are treated as signs of what sort of society exists in the area, rather than as powerful direct influences on governmental behaviour – their analysis 'looks back' to the social system from which they originate. They are also quite different sorts of factor in themselves.

When the age composition of a council is considered, members' length of service must be taken into account. On occasions, discussions during the nomination process have indicated that some potential candidates have thought of themselves as too old to start a 'career'. But no systematic evidence is available about dates of birth, except for the most prominent members, but many of them were young enough to be able to serve for twenty years or more. The main reason why George Lambert was able to serve for 63 years was that he was only 23 when first elected! The predominance of older members, especially in leading positions, reflects the attractiveness of County Council membership once it has been experienced. In every generation Devon County Council has attracted some old individuals but they have generally left through illness or death after relatively short service. Even if they are able councillors they have not been members long enough to build up seniority and acquire leading positions.

One of the reasons why county councillors were on average older than might otherwise have been the case was that 'elevation' to the upper tier often came after service on a district council or involvement in a social, economic or political organisation. The processes by which the status of public person in the county was achieved tended to make 'freshman' councillors relatively old, as they had to serve at district or parish level first and may have had to wait for a 'vacancy' to occur for a considerable time. Secondly, the incumbency factor operates to make promotion slow within the council itself, so that newcomers have to wait a long time to achieve promotion within the system. It is noticeable how many of the long-serving councillors were not 'retired' when they were first recruited to the council but grew old in its service.

It is not therefore surprising that, for instance, in the postwar period Devon County Council (32% retired) had a much greater proportion of older members than did the county borough of Exeter (9.6%).

Women were legally disbarred from membership of county councils until 1907, and in fact the first female candidate did not appear in Devon County Council elections until 1925, the first was elected in 1931 and by the end of 1939 there had been only five women members of the County Council, one of whom had been defeated after three years.

With the advent of universal suffrage women made up just over 50% of the electorate and any council with a proportion of less that a half exhibits under-representation. In the mid-1960s the percentage of women council members in England and Wales as a whole was about 13%, and some areas in the south east and midlands had 20% or even 30%.

In Devon the position began to change after the Second World War. 8.5% of candidates in 1946 were women and though the proportion dropped in the 1950s it appeared in the 1960s to have settled down to about 10% of candidates and a similar proportion of members. But at the first elections for the new system the situation changed dramatically: 22% of candidates and 18% of those elected were women. Since that time women have established themselves as a substantial minority on the County Council and have increasingly taken positions of status and influence, including the Chair and membership of leading committees.

There is no evidence that the reason for so few women candidates after 1907 was that there was an electoral bias against them. It is hard to test for such a factor directly because in the circumstances the 'screening' done by the electorate was invisible. The absence of multi-seat divisions and the varying patterns of candidature make the calculation of electoral performance impossible.

84

	number of women in elections and on the County Council in the years of ordinary elections															
	1931	34	37	46	49	52	55	58	61	64	67	70	73	77	81	85
candidates	2	3	4	12	13	6	6	4	5	14	10	9	63	50	69	63
members	1	2	3	8	10	6	6	8	7	14	12	10	18	19	17	18
total membership	102	102	112	112	112	110	118	118	121	121	121	100	98	98	98	85

The geography behind politics

Political conflict moulds the recruitment process but not necessarily in a highly determinate and predictable way. It may either stabilise or destabilise the membership of an elected body.

In pre-reorganisation Devon some forms of political conflict had a geographical basis. One of the most salient factors in the recruitment process was *place*. By 'place' is meant the residence, or possibly the place of work, of the individual. The County recognised the existence of smaller areas within its boundaries as being of major administrative and financial importance, and therefore politically significant. In county political culture Devon was conceived of as first being divided into broad 'regions', North, West, East and South, with occasional references to 'sub-regions' such as Torbay and the South Hams. Secondly, it was divided into poor law unions which embraced both rural and urban areas. Finally, it was divided into towns and villages – some of which were in legal terms districts and others parishes – and these provided a point of origin for most potential candidates.

Members, including aldermen, were expected to represent definite places within the county. Aldermen were thought of in regional or sub-regional terms but councillors generally had to have some definite connection with the division for which they sought election. However, residence in the same union was sometimes treated as a satisfactory qualification, and individuals did move to neighbouring divisions within its boundaries. It therefore provided a general constraint which reduced 'carpet-bagging' to a negligible role.

Place, however, was also a cause of political conflict. It was one source of contested aldermanic by-elections as different regions argued that the vacancy should go to someone from their area. Some divisions were mixed urban and rural areas and there was sometimes argument that the constituency should be represented by the 'other' part. Similarly the bi- or tri-centred divisions consisting of two or more villages or small towns of nearly equal size required successful candidates to transcend the parish or the ward in which they lived if they were not to face repeated challenges. If an individual could do this then, because the number of possible rivals was a relatively small group (of district councillors), amongst whom there is a considerable degree of information flow, it was possible to avoid the greater competitiveness that introduced more uncertainty into the system.

The importance of this factor was attested by ambivalence over the nature of representation: was the division better off represented by a powerful person, for instance the largest landowner, or by someone who understood ordinary people? Both attitudes played a part in the recruitment process.

However, not all 'places' were equally well represented. Devon was a county of hamlets, villages and small towns, with only a few medium-sized urban areas. The social geography of Devon was accurately reflected in its un-reformed district and parish structure; thus small town and rural Devon had more political and administrative leaders than they could expect on crude quantitative grounds. The electoral system reinforced this. As is common in Britain, rural areas tended to be over-represented when electoral divisions were created; population decline, in some cases absolute as well as relative, allied with an inertia in boundaries, tended to increase this.

Religion

Victorian and Edwardian national politics were strongly influenced by religious divisions within society and it is not surprising that the differences between Anglicans and non-conformists should be a major factor in local politics. Three issues stood out as dividing politicians at local level on religious lines: tithes, the role of the established church in state education, and the problem of alcoholic drink.

The religious affiliation of candidates was as well-known as their partisan-ship. It was regarded as a legitimate matter for public political comment and relevant to the recruitment process, in ways that are remininiscent today more of Northern Ireland than of Greater London. The most obvious sign of religious affiliation is being a minister of religion and this was a noticeable category on the County Council during the period studied. For those who were not ministers their participation in their chosen religion was often reported in the local press, as was their involvement in temperance organ-isations, tithe and rate strikes and controversies over school government. I have found no reports of militantly non-religious candidates but presumably there were some who took their formal religion lightly.

Echoes of this religious division continued into the 1920s and 1930s. But the temperance and educational issues were becoming less important and though they could reappear at any moment they did not have the public prominence that they had before 1914. The decline in salience continued in the postwar period but never entirely disappeared. Particularly in north and west Devon nonconformity remained relatively strong but it is very difficult to get hard evidence about the religious backgrounds of candidates and members.

Class and social status

It must be remarked at the beginning that the working and lower middle classes were almost completely unrepresented during the early periods, even at the level of candidature. I have found only one indisputably working-class candidate before 1914 – and he withdrew before the election – and a few 'possibles'. But most were undoubtedly middle or upper class by any obvious test. Reorganisation has not greatly increased the proportion of working-class members but this is partly because of the weakness of the Labour Party in Devon. Political conflict based on economic interest and social differences was more important than the broad class divisions of the national political system.

The *class* dimension originally involved several factors that overlapped and intersected. First, there was a major division between the agricultural interest and industry; those dependent on the former were particularly 'class-conscious'. Secondly, there was the rural-urban division already mentioned which was not identical with, but obviously overlapped, the agriculture-industry distinction. Thirdly, there was a 'landed' interest wider than the purely agricultural interest but contrasted with interests based on capital that were themselves wider than those of industry.

Within the major divisions there was further differentiation based on economic status. The most noticeable of these was in agriculture where the difference between owner-occupiers and tenants was regarded as highly significant. The scale of enterprise involved in industry was also a distinctive factor within the non-agricultural sector; commerce seemed to have been the occupation of many of the smaller 'capitalists'.

For this period there is the need also to use the concept of *social status* in addition to that of *economic class*. The newspaper reporting of local politics makes it clear that there are many subtle gradations of status within each category, particularly the more important ones. The connections of this factor with *family* and *public service* seem clear. Occupation of a 'principal seat', possession of one of the historic Devon names, an aristocratic title or a baronetcy, success in public life – these help to define a high status and public regard which modifies crude economic well-being as a measure of social differentiation.

Incumbency and public service

The mechanism that connects all the separate factors in an enduring system is *incumbency*. This involved three aspects of behaviour: a willingness to seek re-election and to continue for a long period, lack of opposition if seeking re-election and the chance to be elected an alderman. Before 1973 the over-whelmingly significant facts about the membership as individuals were their strong connections with the public life of the county and their long-term commitment to the County Council as an organisation. This commitment was a very personal matter and arose partly from service itself. The County Council shared some of the features of French Third and Fourth Republic legislatures – it was a 'house without windows', or in British terms 'the best club' in the area. It thus very effectively socialised many newcomers into the system and made them want to continue as members.

There were of course no incumbents in the first election in 1889 but some individuals had high social status and public reputations which led those interested in the new body to treat them as virtually sure of election if they wished to serve. The result was that the first County Council was a very impressive body by the standards of the time. It included many of the leaders of Quarter Sessions, a number of prominent 'newcomers', a noticeable contingent of Parliamentarians (serving, former and would-be), a substantial aristocratic element and even more gentry, and a number who had written and lectured extensively about public affairs, including county government.

From that time onwards incumbency played a major part in the political system of the County Council. For instance, it enhanced the political power of rural Devon by the greater stability of its 'delegations' to the County Council. As size of 'community' increased serving members became less willing to seek re-election, the percentage of contested elections increased, the proportion of partisan candidatures increased and generally the elections became more competitive. For instance, in the period after the Second World War, out of the 736 elections the serving member was re-elected in 572 (78%) and was defeated in only 7.6%. These aggregate figures however conceal differences between areas. If electoral divisions are grouped according to the status of the lower-tier authority in their location, a clear distinction can be seen between those that are entirely within a rural district (17.5% contested) and those that are entirely or partly within an urban area (37% contested). The inertial force of incumbency was strengthened by the over-representation of small communities. Only 20% of members left the council through defeat at an election, the same proportion that was called by the Great Elector Death. Quantitatively the most significant cause of ceasing to be a member was through not seeking re-election, but this is an unsatisfactory general category as it includes some who faced prospective defeat and others who were seriously ill or dying.

The persistence of serving members had one major mechanical influence on the process of recruitment; it created a 'pushback' effect which implanted an inertia in the system and acted as a 'memory' of past systems, carrying the influences of previous years into the present and future. New members, and therefore new types of people, cannot enter the system if serving members do not leave. Thus old socio-political conflicts were carried from decade to decade in the persons of the long-serving members. There was always a considerable number of members who were originally recruited in an earlier phase or epoch of the council's history – and were presumably socialised in part much earlier than that. Each decade in fact contributed its share to the council leadership but as time passed this decreased in significance. In the daily work of the council new members were always a minority and had to work themselves gradually into important positions in the operational structure of the authority.

The first and fourth periods, however, were somewhat different. Before the First World War the political conflicts mentioned above made all divisions equally likely (or unlikely) to experience changes in representation. After reorganisation partisanship created a degree of homogeneity across the geographical spectrum, extending to the size of electoral divisions.

The period from 1946 to 1972 is the most interesting because of its transitional nature. It is clear that the differentiated society that was the foundation of the traditional county government had not passed away in Devon in the late 1940s. The traditional descriptions of rural and small-town society still dominated the composition of the county council. Though there is no good evidence on this point one would hazard a guess that the processes of social change (based on economic change) which occurred in the midlands and south east and in the urban areas of the north many years ago have been taking place in Devon only in the last 30 years. These changes were eventually reflected in a changing composition of local councils, but because of the inertia of the system the latter changed relatively slowly.

The fragility of the system was obvious. It could be endangered by a rise in competitiveness generally and by the failure of socialisation processes in the council itself to 'lock' the successful candidate in a position favourable to council service. The reactions of new elected members to their first period of council service and the treatment they receive are vital parts of the interaction between council and environment. Though it is difficult to be very sure, it is probable that reorganisation, which changed the basis of political recruitment, came just in time to save the reputation of the traditional system in Devon County Council.

The electoral process and the formation of cohorts

As there can be no leaders without followers the study of political leadership requires an analysis of the changing combinations of 'freshmen' and 'oldstagers' and the 'maturing' of each group of entrants to the elected body. A *cohort* consists of all individuals who entered the council for the first time at a given date or during a defined period, in this analysis those elected at one ordinary election and the by-elections held before the next. From the moment it is formed a cohort can only lose members but the speed at which it does so is an important factor in the working of a leadership system. The long-term stability of a council, however, depends on a process of renewal as well as a process of persistence. A well balanced council has a mixture of long-, medium- and short-service members, the last providing the necessary element of flexibility in the system. Elections are occasions for opting out of a system, as well as opportunities for new types of person to enter. How far did each election and each period produce its 'quota' of members who would serve for different lengths of time? How far were replacements similar to departing members? The development of successive cohort 'profiles' reflects the circumstances under which each was formed.

For the first 80 years Devon County Council depended on enoh suitable candidates putting themselves forward, or being pushed forward by others, to enable sufficient leaders to be found amongst its members. 'Screening' by the electorate was of little direct importance because of the prevalence of uncontested elections and the role of the aldermanic system. But once reorganisation came and contested elections became universal within the County Council the electorate began to affect the composition of the membership by the way, in aggregate, it cast its votes. Forces in the environment, particularly those of social change, can affect local councils gradually and imperceptibly over the years by a process akin to osmosis, but elections have a potential for drama when changes outside the body may suddenly make a marked incursion into its heart. This potential for sudden change was not, however, realised in Devon until 1973 and the influence of elections was almost entirely stabilising and conservative in a social sense, though not in terms of the impact of government on the citizen.

Even in very stable times a proportion of the Council were 'freshmen'. Until

1973 this largely depended upon what participants and observers often called a 'vacancy' occurring, that is, a retiring member not seeking re-election. A second source of change was the willingness of non-members to challenge incumbents; this sometimes caused the retiring member not to seek re-election and sometimes he or she was defeated in the poll. The third source of new members was the creation of new seats, either through a redistribution of divisions or the addition of extra seats. This played a minor part in Devon until local government reorganisation; gains occurred at the elections of 1910 (one), 1925 (two), 1937 (seven), 1955 (six) and 1961 (two). Seats, and therefore members, were lost in 1901 (one), 1913–19 (three), 1952 (one) and 1966–1968 (16). In each case the consequent aldermanic changes slightly increased the size of the changes upwards and downwards.

'Promotion Within the Council'

The analysis now turns to 'life experiences' within the Council itself because these account for the willingness of individuals to seek re-election and thus for the stability of a cohort and continuity within the Council.

The formation of cohorts depended on an interaction between electoral behaviour and 'life' on the Council. The explanation of the willingness of incumbents to seek re-election almost indefinitely can only be found in the attraction of Council membership. The existence of the committee system and extensive rights of nomination to other public bodies ensured that all members could play a distinctive part in the operation of the local authority. The individual could develop 'bespoke' roles for him- or herself and it was easy to recognise that seniority was rewarded by 'promotion' within the system. Committee work created respect and friendliness between members so that involvement in decision-making was a satisfying personal experience as well as a contribution to developments that were important to the County.

In newly created bodies the first leaders must come from outside the system. In such cases external abilities, status and power play a part in determining which of many possible individuals actually achieve the 'top' positions within the organisation. Once the first distinct period has passed it becomes possible for members to achieve high office through their activities within its boundaries or in representational roles towards the outside world. Institutionalisation in this sense happened to Devon County Council rather slowly but by 1914 its boundaries were clear and entry was governed by factors which tended to discourage non-system-oriented candidates. A large proportion of members, once elected, were reluctant to leave before they had accumulated considerable periods of service. In their first years, however, the council newcomers were definitely treated as 'freshmen' and expected to work themselves up the scale through its power and status systems. The process can best be thought of as 'promotion' and depends on some individuals valuing responsibility more than others.

For council members the local authority contains a working system based on committees, subcommittees of various types, relations with officials, relations with satellites' and 'associates', and interaction with other public agencies. For Devon County Council the easily quantifiable aspects of this system have been described in the previous chapter. The County Council needed members willing to serve on sufficient committees and sub-committees to spread the work around, and also willing to serve as nominees to other bodies. If an individual accepted less than the average number of memberships and appointments then others had to take on more work. Even in the early years it became evident that some individuals were taking on more committee memberships and roles than were other members and efforts were made to spread responsibility and workloads more equally. But ultimately no-one can force a council member to accept nomination and to actually attend meetings if he or she does not wish to do so.

Differential participation is therefore the key first stage of the promotion process. Members who wished to advance within the system had to take on their fair share of duties and carry them out properly in a manner which would impress fellow members. The standing-committee system was an essential stage for this type of behaviour and also provided a basis for interventions at full Council meetings.

Leadership positions

Each part of the system also needed its own leaders in the form of a chairman and vice- or deputy chairman. It was advantageous to the County Council if its representatives took leading positions on outside bodies. Willingness to take on extra responsibility marked out the members who could expect to progress in the system. This is the second stage of the promotion process.

However, the promotion process shared one factor with the electoral process; incumbency played the same 'pushback' role in the allocation to roles as it did in creating 'vacancies' in ordinary elections. In general, unless they were willing to challenge the prevailing conventions, individuals could only move upwards if others stood down. Within the Council this factor tended to be referred to as 'seniority' and length of service – an easily measurable characteristic – was clearly relevant to promotion.

Incumbency and seniority are obviously non-subjective or universal rules of allocation and promotion but there is also clear evidence that in Devon other factors operated from time to time, and these introduced a degree of subjectivity into the process. The allocation process became less automatic because each of the other factors was a more complex judgemental attribute and because the existence of multiple criteria made weighting a necessary action. The other factors clearly taken into account on some occasions at least are 'relevance', 'locality', and 'ability' or 'merit'. Even if in principle each of these latter criteria are universal in practice there is ample scope for disagreement about their impact in individual cases. In effect they involve evaluating peers publicly, something that automatic decision-rules avoid.

Further research is needed on these points, particularly to try to discover what sort of circumstances evoke one pattern of behaviour and what are associated with others. Also it is desirable to study committee transfers between years, as 'voting with one's feet' is one of the best indicators of a preference system. The analysis of promotion within the committee system is difficult because systemic factors interact with personal preferences. It is however clear that committees differed markedly in the proportion of seniors to juniors in their membership.

The Committee System in 1960
seniority index [= total number of years served divided by number of committee members]

20+ years	1 Joint Staff (22.6)
16–19 years	4 Standing Joint (18.5), Finance (17.1), Establishment (16.7), Legal & General Purposes (16.5)
14–15 years	2 Dartmoor National Park (15.8), Estates (14.2)
12–13 years	7 Diseases of Animals (13.8), Smallholdings (13.4), Roads (13.3), Education (12.9), Coastal Protection (12.8), Local Taxation (12.1), Water & Sanitation (12.0)
9–11 years	3 Planning (11.0), Welfare (9.9), Health (9.1)
less than 9 years	3 Children (7.6), Plympton Redevelopment (6.8), Supplies (5.6)

As with most other councils the positions of committee chairman and vice-chairman were of special importance. The first sign of this is the dominance of aldermen in these offices. In addition, senior members as measured by length of service occupied most of the offices. The testimony of members themselves provides evidence of the process at work. The important stage was election as vice-chairman of a committee, which was partly a result of 'good' service on it. The expectation then was that eventually when the chairman stepped down, usually at a time of his or her own choosing, the vice-chairman would succeed. When this did not happen there was ill-feeling but the long term consequences could be ultra-stability and this occasionally provoked protests from relative newcomers.

Length of Council Service of Chairmen and Vice-Chairmen, 1960		
length of service	chairmen	vice-chairmen
less than 6 years	2	3
6–9 inclusive	1	3
10–14 inclusive	2	2
15–19 inclusive	5	4
20–24 inclusive	1	6
25–29 inclusive	4	3
30+ years	7	—

Before reorganisation, committees chose their own leaders and it therefore paid the 'ambitious' member to specialise. Individuals had some power to determine which committees they would join, though there was a general expectation that the different 'regions' of Devon would all be represented to some extent on each. In 1973 power to allocate to committees and to appoint chairmen and vice-chairmen passed to the party groups; hence the 'life' of the committee itself became less important to the promotion of the individual. Even when the system of 'technical chairmanships' was implemented at the annual meeting in 1988, as a consequence of a lack of a 'government' within the Council, the distribution of portfolios was negotiated outside the committees themselves. It may be that similar factors operate within the meetings of party members but these are not visible to the outsider.

The aldermanic system

The aldermanic system in the pre-reorganisation Council is the best illustration of the role of status and promotion within the system.

Though councils had the right to elect anyone qualified to be a councillor as alderman, in most areas this office was regarded as a promotion or reward for service and was therefore restricted to those who were already councillors. In the early years high status 'outsiders' were often elected to the aldermanic bench but after 1910 this practice died out and invariably councillors were 'promoted' when a vacancy arose. The extent to which prior service was treated as a qualification can be seen from the experience of the postwar years. Of the 28 aldermen in 1946 only 3 had less than ten years and 18 had 15 or more years service before being elected to the office. There is also impressionistic evidence from the elections themselves to suggest that this was a major factor in the culture of the council. The aldermanic office also tended to be for life in that incumbents were virtually always re-elected if they wished. The two exceptions were in the unusual circumstances of the 1968 'clean sweep' election necessitated by the loss of Torbay from the county. In virtually every election there was at least 20% difference in the support for the least popular incumbent as compared with the most popular newcomer.

Aldermen were therefore in a good position to make a long-term contribution to the Council's leadership system. In 1973 the great majority of holders of the position on the County Council had been members for more than 28 years.

The chairmen of the Council

The position of chairman of the Council needs special analysis because this was a post to which most members could not aspire and therefore recruitment to that position was governed by other factors. The role has changed several times during the hundred years. In formal terms the two distinct periods since 1973 are the most clearly differentiated from the earlier ones but there is evidence that the position in relation to the older County Council changed gradually in the first fifty years.

In terms of the conventions of the local constitution the rule applied that once in office both chairman and vice-chairmen were re-elected unopposed. When a chairman insisted on stepping down, something that the Council was sometimes reluctant to accept, the vice-chairman was promoted without opposition. The real decision was the choice of new vice-chairman, as in 1889, 1946 and 1955.

The most important fact about the early chairmen was that they were of high social and economic status. The impression given is that it was important that Baron Clinton (1889–1901), the Earl of Morley (1901–1904) and Earl Fortescue (1904–1916) – formerly Lord Ebrington – were peers of the realm and could represent the Council socially. Sir T. H. Hepburn (1916) was the first of the

93

newcomers of 1889 to achieve the highest office but unfortunately by the time he succeeded he was old and ill and almost immediately had to resign.

The chairmanship of Sir Henry Lopes (1916–1938), later Lord Roborough, marks the transition from the social leader specification of the role to the working 'headship' of the elected side of the authority. The practice was adopted of putting the chairman ex-officio on all committees and including him in the delegation to the County Councils' Association. His election illustrates the need of the system for someone actually able to do a demanding job, and he undoubtedly presided over very difficult times. Sir John Daw (1938–1946), who had a strong individual character, confirmed the new role and the position became one which led to social recognition for the hard work it involved. The impression is given that ten years was long enough for one man to hold the office: hence Sir John Shelley (1946–1955), Sir G. C. Hayter-Hames (1955–65), John A. Day (1965–66, died), Gerald Whitmarsh (1966–1971), and Colonel J. E. Palmer (1971–end, tenure ended by reorganisation).

The Conservative preference after 1973 was for a tenure corresponding to the four-year 'life' of a council, but the Alliance preferred the annual system which had operated in most boroughs for the mayoral office. After twelve years of Conservative dominance, with Councillors C. A. Ansell, G. E. H. Creber and A. L. Goodrich (after H. S. Sargent's death in office) having four years each, there were successively Liberal (D. G. Potter), Labour (W. E. Evans), Alliance (Mrs E. Stacey, the first woman 'chairman'), and A. L. Sayers (Conservative). It is clear that the position of 'Leader of the Council', which is now an official title, is the one that corresponds most closely to the role of pre-reorganisation council chairman.

Administrative Leadership

The roles of senior officers can be analysed in ways that are very similar to those used for council members but differences arise from the nature of appointment as opposed to election.

First, corresponding to the cohort of members is the *generation* of officers. The tenure of staff is not structured by a pattern of three- or four-year 'blocs' and a simultaneous mass start and finish to office-holding does not occur. But those who enter the employment of a local authority during the same distinct period can be thought of as a generation because they share some things in common and are part of the same process. Secondly, the status system within the ranks of the staff depends partly on the standing of occupations in the outside world. Lawyers, bankers and accountants, doctors, surveyors and architects belong to well-established professions whilst educational administrators, social administrators and social workers, librarians, public health and consumer-protection workers belong to occupations largely created by the local government system itself. In the postwar period the assimilation of planning staff and management specialists has posed similar problems to those experienced by the heads of 'new' services in the early twentieth century.

Thirdly, the power of individual chief officers is influenced by the role and size of the department they head. The heads of the 'horizontal' departments, such as those responsible for legal and secretarial work, finance and, in recent years, specialised administrative techniques, have an impact well beyondthe boundaries of their own organisation because they are involved in aspects of the work of all other departments. The best examples of this were the Clerk's and Treasurer's 'departments'. The size of department in terms of staff and expenditure can also be a factor but the significance then derives from the impact of the activities on the outside world. The Education Department since 1902 is a good example of the latter. Education is local government's most expensive service and involves a large staff of both professionals and administrators. Since compulsory school attendance it has had very high visibility in society and in modern times it is very important in the individual's life. Education has tended everywhere to become an 'authority within the authority'.

But as with elected members there was also the *individuality* factor. Within the framework imposed by the system of departments individuals could make a contribution to the development of the local authority through their own personality and energy. Particularly in the early years the County Council depended on a few individual chief officers for the modernisation of its services and the expansion of its role in local society.

The Careers of Chief Officers

The career pattern for senior employees differs from that of elected members because it may involve changing employers as well as upwards promotion within the system. Inter-authority mobility depends on the existence of nationally recognised occupational categories, differences in pay according to size of authority and differences in the desirability of living in some areas rather than others.

Individual local authorities by themselves can do little about the evolution of country-wide local government professions. In the twentieth century specific local government occupations have gradually organised themselves, introduced tests of professional competence and successfully pressed for the creation of national grading schemes which reduce the discretion and autonomy of individual employers. Devon's record in this respect was until the 1950s generally one of resistance and eventual reluctant acceptance of national developments.

As a medium-sized county Devon had scope for attracting ambitious officers as part of the individual's career strategy. This factor would point to a flow of well-qualified young to middle-aged professionals through the authority. However, Devon was and is an area where individuals prefer to live; all public services, including the educational sector, tend to have less difficulty in attracting and retaining staff than less favoured parts of the country. The result was that during the period of consolidation and expansion the County Council's departments were led by a number of long-serving chief officers. The policy of appointing deputies to succeed chief officers increased the length of tenure of many individuals.

Headquarters organisation

The centre of any department is constituted by its headquarters staff. One of the main developments was the development of the chief officer system which was largely in the first instance 'imposed' on a decentralised system of indirect administration. As new services were added new chief officers were appointed. From the mid-Edwardian period onwards the Council minutes and reports chart the gradual increase in complexity at central level as a deputy chief officer was appointed in department after department, then assistant chief officers, senior professional officers and so on.

However, the development of administrative leadership at the local authority level, in addition to within departments, was retarded by two factors. First, the scattering of departmental headquarters throughout Exeter, which was described earlier, encouraged separate thinking and action in respect of individual services. Secondly, the straightforward 'taking over' of the arrangements for the clerkship and treasurership from Quarter Sessions was a mistake and caused problems for decades. It is impossible to reconstruct the realities of co-ordination but the Clerk's organisation was clearly a source of great concern to members in the Edwardian period. After a very awkward few years in the 1890s the National Provincial Bank became the Treasurer's 'department' and this association did not come to an end until March, 1948, when the treasurer's duties were merged with those of the accountant and chief financial officer to produce a Treasurer's Department solely within the local authority.

Probably the crucial period for the clerk's role was the tenure of Brian S. Miller from 1914 to 1937. In 1906 and 1909 there were great difficulties and talk of a possible 'breakdown' in the Council's central administration. The man who appears to have being doing all the internal managerial and financial work within the Clerk's Department was first appointed to a new position of Deputy Clerk and then became Clerk for two years (1912–14) after a long career with Quarter Sessions and the County Council. At that time the Council began to systematise the second level of management within the Department and A. J. Withycombe became Chief Accounting Officer as well as a Deputy Clerk in September, 1915.

Since that time the Clerk's Department has grown in size and complexity. For a considerable time it was also the finance department (as distinct from the treasurership) but this function was separated from the other business of the Department in 1948, as described above. There is little doubt that the Clerkship of H. G. Godsall (1952–72) confirmed the Department as being at the centre of the County Council's administrative leadership. The next development was the creation of a Chief Executive role without the headship of major administrative agencies. With the appointment of D. G. Macklin the Council moved to the alternative 'Bains' system, in which a number of major functions were made the direct responsibility of the Chief Executive, and the Secretary's Department was abolished.

Membership of the 'management team'

In 1948 the principle of the 'big five' was reaffirmed. These were the Clerk, Treasurer, Surveyor, Chief Education Officer and Medical Officer of Health. As the 1950s progressed there was an increase in the number of 'principal officers' and meetings of them began to be called on a regular basis. It is impossible to determine how important general chief officers' meetings were, even who attended and what, if anything, was decided.

Another feature of the postwar period was the introduction of the policy of listing the deputy chief officers of some departments as 'principal officers' of the Council. The implication of this is that the Deputy Clerk, Treasurer, Medical Officer and Education Officer were as important as the Architect, Valuer/Land Agent, Planning Officer, Chief Fire Officer etc.

As with many other authorities Devon formalised the above system at reorganisation. The leading chief officers are now denoted in the Yearbook as members of the Management Team. In 1987–88 these were the Chief Executive, National Park Officer, Chief Education Officer, Engineer and Planning Officer, Chief Fire Officer, Librarian, Manpower Services Officer, Director of Property, Director of Social Services, Supplies Officer, Trading Standards Officer and Treasurer.

The Overall Management System

The overall management system depends on the relations between elected members and appointed officers. It has been seen that Devon County Council started as a relatively simple organisation and has become increasingly more complex during the hundred years. Its officer structure developed towards greater elaboration, and there was an increasing tendency to make use of modern management techniques. The committee system settled down into a regular pattern drawn out systematically. Relations with outside bodies were also systematised by formal agreements covering exchange of members through co-option and nomination arrangements.

One of the main aspects of the overall management system was delegation to officers. This affected finance and staffing in particular. But consideration must also be given to the general style and tone of relations between council members and all employees.

Delegation to officers

Delegation to officers occurs in two ways. First, since 1974 it may be deliberate in the sense that the full council meeting or a committee may discuss and then vote on a resolution to permit a named officer to carry out duties without further reference to the council or committee. This is easy to document because it will be recorded in the relevant minutes but it is relatively rare because it is generally unnecessary.

One reason for this is that many chief officers have a sort of statutory position which requires them to act on their own initiative in certain cirumstances. Chief constables, medical officers of health, treasurers and clerks to councils, for instance, all had responsibilities which, if they failed to discharge them, could lead to personal blame. Council members quickly get into the habit of expecting chief officers to take many actions without specific reference to the elected representatives. In sociological terms local authority departments are bureaucracies and they carry out a large amount of routine business without any difficulty. Chief officers are responsible for the smooth running of the organisation which they head and they do not generally need any guidance or assistance from elected members with this function.

The second kind of delegation is therefore the *de facto* handing over of the power to determine matters to employees, because there are too many issues to be decided by council members, even if that was thought desirable. The same process has produced delegated legislation, administrative tribunals and field office decision-making in central government.

Delegation to officers increased dramatically in the twentieth century. Though it is difficult to reconstruct the nineteenth century situation it appears that in the early years of county councils it was thought to be either legally difficult or unreasonable to leave some matters to officers. It was also the case that there were few officers to whom delegation could be made. The result was that many actions that would be taken or originated by officers today were carried out by council members. The cases of *management* within the County Council and *finance* will be used to illustrate this point.

Management within the local authority

Local authorities are complex organisations because they contain two types of dramatis personae – elected and appointed – and are responsible for a range of distinct public services. Local authority decision-making has always been dominated by problems of co-ordination: between council members and officers, between separate committees and between separate departments.

From earliest days the County Council has recognised the importance of administrative efficiency and effectiveness and like most local authorities of the time developed an indigenous tradition of dealing with problems of co-ordination within its own 'walls'. Many council members took an interest in these matters and produced proposals for organisational change from their own resources.

But as more chief officers came to be appointed there was created another source of administrative reform. Each chief officer tended to try to build up his own organisation as an efficient entity and proposals for change within departments increasingly came from their heads.

Eventually the growth of individual departments led to a recognition of the problems of relations between departments and this necessitated an increase in the powers of the 'horizontal' chief officers, particularly the clerk and the treasurer. As a result of the expansion of county council services in the 1940s the matter became acute and since that time administrative efficiency has rarely been off the agenda.

Three changes started to take place in the 1960s. The first was a purely linguistic one: councils all over the country starting talking about 'management' rather than 'administration' and Devon was no exception. Management became a fashion which has lasted to the present day. Secondly, the number of 'horizontal' departments began to increase with the appointment of senior officers with standard management functions. Thirdly, insularity began to decline and councils increasingly recognised that what was happening in other authorities, other public bodies and the private sector contained valuable lessons for the individual council in its search for more efficient and effective organisation.

Thus questions of internal organisation have become a subject that is as professionalised as direct service provision. Devon has been thoroughly 'managerialised' and this will continue into the foreseeable future.

Finance

The County Council started life with only an elementary financial administration. The duties of the treasurer, which were narrowly specified by law, were carried out by a senior member of the National Provincial Bank, whilst the Clerk to the council had one assistant to help with this function. But a number of council members took a great interest in financial matters and may be said to have specialised in the subject. There has been a continuous input from the elected representative side of the authority into the financial process but its nature has changed over the decades.

Perhaps because of their backgrounds as large-property owners, many members seem to have had an understanding of complex financial matters and played a role in the formulating of policies in this sphere. Others stood for the 'economical' tradition in local government which stresses the need for eternal vigilance against waste and over-spending by local authorities. This group appealed to the condition of ratepayers and sought always to reduce the 'burdens' on them.

As time passed, however, the Council increasingly came to rely on officers holding newly created positions to undertake the financial planning and calculation that the growth of central grants entailed. The 'backwoodsmen' still played their parts in the processes but the starting point of the annual financial system became the analysis done by the treasurer's department. As the grant system has changed in recent years so financial perspectives have become longer, the exploitation of 'resources' more complicated and the technical competence of the financial staff much greater.

The key change occurred with the reform of the grant system in 1929. Before this date the Council was largely concerned with the calculation of a 'fair' precept and the minimisation of 'burdens' on districts and parishes. Since then the grant element as a source of local income has become more complicated with each successive central–local financial system. It is vital that expert advice be available about the impact of each aspect of the grant system on Devon, irrespective of its impact elsewhere. It has been necessary to lengthen the time needed for financial decisions so that the budgetary process now has to begin in effect before the previous cycle has finished. The Treasurer is a key figure in interpreting the outside world to the County Council, often warning members about the probable consequences of central government changes in the grant system and related matters.

Council member-officer relations

De facto delegation emerges from council member–officer relationships. Decision-making within a local authority involves complicated processes through which the decision and its elements pass, involving sometimes members only and sometimes officers only, and sometimes both together.

This may be illustrated by a reading of the County Council minutes at every period in its history. Business can be divided into many different categories. Much routine information, for instance reports on agricultural diseases and weights and measures inspections, has come before the Council. At the opposite end the problem of Dartmoor is unique to Devon, though it shares some features with other areas of 'outstanding natural beauty'. Implementing superannuation legislation was a task which the County had to do but it did so reluctantly, and dealing with individual officers raised general questions which the members took a long time to solve. The planning and building of the new County Hall illustrates the difficulties of members appreciating the role of the working conditions of employees. Promoting economic development – the function of the 1980s – unites both members and officers in spirit, whilst implementing 'privatisation' legislation was potentially, but not actually, extremely divisive.

It will be clear from these examples that the relations between members and officers can vary almost infinitely. It is, however, important to make some generalisations about the respective roles of each.

First, compared with central government and appointed bodies, the existence of council members guarantees publicity for local authority decision-making: publicity within the complex organisation, publicity for other public bodies and publicity for outside interests and the private citizen. Because matters come before meetings and are recorded in documents this function will be fulfilled irrespective of whether council members 'really' decide issues or not. However it is well known that information is not always acquired, noticed or appreciated by those who are affected by it. Hence Devon eventually appointed a press officer whose work in fact increases the extent to which the three categories [other 'insiders', other bodies and the general public] can gain knowledge of what is going on. The function of dealing with the outside world – including central government, the local authority associations and the European Community – has become more important for officers with the passage of time. Unfortunately there is no space to deal with this in detail.

Secondly, even when most business is transacted at committee and council meetings 'on the nod', the elected-representative stage permits another look at difficult, controversial and possibly wrongly decided issues. Meetings do in fact often involve the re-consideration of provisional decisions, and this is valuable even if the original outcome is confirmed. Every year produces examples of this type of business before the full Council.

Thirdly, it is possible for new types and items of business to enter the system via the actions of elected representatives. This function is one of the most difficult to illustrate confidently because so many of the possible elements in it are invisible at the time and, if not, are quickly lost as days, months and years pass.

Fourthly, only council members can ultimately resolve serious disputes between departments and chief officers. I have not come across evidence in Devon of the type of serious dispute which occasionally in other individual authorities has led chief officers not to speak to each other. But it can be seen that, if there is conflict, only elected representatives can decide the relative status, reflected in differential salaries, of chief officer posts and, when reorganisations take place, which department absorbs and which is absorbed.

Officers also make a distinctive contribution to the decision-making process. First, they are responsible for seeing that decision-making is founded on a sound technical basis, that is, whatever professional and scientific considerations are relevant are brought to bear at every stage. Secondly, they are responsible for trying to ensure that the council's decisions are within the law. Members often to want to do things that are not within their powers ('ultra vires'), not because they deliberately wish to break the law but because they are not legal experts. An extension of this role includes finding ways of doing what the council wants without acting illegally.

Thirdly, they are responsible for the details of administration, which often involve acting away from headquarters and often outside the council buildings altogether, and dealing with outside groups and members of the public on a day-to-day basis.

Fourthly, they are responsible for initiating innovations arising partly from deficiencies in existing arrangements, partly from the central government (e.g. new legislation), and partly from professional and scientific developments in the community at large. Most chief officers are members of the relevant local, regional and national professional associations, receive newsletters and journals, and some attend national and international conferences. A few from Devon have played prominent roles as officers of their association.

The Parallel Development of Political and Administrative Leadership

From the end of the Edwardian period onwards the two types of leadership developed in parallel within the County Council. The internal roles of chairman and vice-chairman evolved side-by-side with the enhancing of the position of the 'horizontal' functions of the Clerk's Department. As the 'chief financial officer's' role became more important so did that of the Finance Committee chairman. As more 'horizontal' functions were recognised in the 1950s and 1960s specialist officers were appointed to provide them and specialist committees or subcommittees to support and supervise them.

At the level of the individual participant the practice grew up of having vice-chairmen succeed chairmen and deputies succeed chief officers. The result was that at the head of every major service and activity there was a 'team' of four – two officers and two council members – who were expected to serve for a noticeable length of time but who changed every so often as a result of the natural processes that affect all human beings. The expected was not always realised: sometimes vice-chairmen died before their chairman and ambitious deputies sought promotion outside the County boundaries. Nevertheless the system provided an individual leadership that was stable over noticeable periods of time but changed as circumstances dictated and thus promoted within the system new people and often therefore new types of individual. Providing the right combination of stability and change is probably the most important task of any leadership system in local government. The old Devon did it very well; the new has still to resolve some of its problems.

6

THE PAST AND THE FUTURE

The County Council today and challenges
to its identity

The hundred years of county councils began with pessimism and predictions of the collapse of county administration and it ends with the system of two- and three-tier local government facing attack from several directions. But in 1889 the general problems of local government were less acute in Devon than in many other parts of the country. The 'doomsday' attitudes of some traditional local leaders elsewhere found little real support here, the difficulties created by historic boundaries were few and the relations with the large urban areas within the geographical county settled as quickly as could be expected.

Is it still true that local government in Devon is less troubled than in many other parts of England? Of course if general reform comes as a part of national policy change Devon will experience the same developments as other counties. It has to come to terms with the poll tax, uniform business rates and a changing system of central grants, and if the centre so decides it will join the Greater London Council, Rutland and the West Riding in some local government 'heaven'. But there is nothing in its history that provides good arguments for sweeping reorganisation of local government.

One direction of possible change in local government is towards larger areas in the form of regional and subregional government. The submerging of Devon in a Greater South Western Region based on Bristol would be very strongly opposed by public authorities and political leaders and would receive equally strong opposition from Cornwall. 'Regionalisation' of local government has no advantages for the 'Far South West' and fortunately it does not appear to be on the national political agenda. But because of its peninsular nature the far south west is more vulnerable to proposals for subregional

102

government since this could be achieved in the area by a simple merger of Devon and Cornwall which would not be open to the same objections as face a Bristol-based large 'province'. However, the 'subregionalisation' of English government is also not a serious item on the present political agenda, although it might become a contender if certain other developments took place.

These 'other developments' are to be found in the pressures from below for an enhancement of the role of districts in local government. The effect of the 1971–74 reorganisation was to leave the lower tier with relatively few services – the non-metropolitan county is 'top-heavy' in terms of 'weight' in the system – which was not a serious downgrading for the small boroughs, urban and rural districts of the traditional pattern but which led to a considerable loss of local control in the former county boroughs. Almost before the new system was in operation it was challenged by the larger urban areas who sought 'organic change' through a transfer of some county council services to the dozen largest districts. This episode ended with the defeat of the Labour Government in 1979 but the general idea has recently been revived by the Association of District Councils in a more extreme form.

District councils argue that county council services can be administered by districts, with joint arrangements where necessary. But realistically it must be recognised that in the 1960s, in the eyes of central government, the minimum population size for major service provision was enlarged dramatically and the 100,000 'plimsoll line' disappeared, almost certainly for ever, to be replaced with levels at least twice that. Though low density of population may justify smaller authorities in some areas, the general position of the centre is that major units of local government must be large. Also joint arrangements are acceptable only if they play a limited role, as in the present metropolitan county areas. They have few reasoned arguments in favour of them and a system dominated by inter-authority organisations would be confusing and potentially inefficient.

The implications of this for Devon are clear. Only Plymouth, with 253,000 inhabitants the fifth largest non-metropolitan district in 1984, qualifies by itself on the population criterion. The other nine districts would have to be merged into three or four new areas, probably with some dismemberment of existing units as the first stage. This is not what the smaller districts in general appear to want and has no obvious advantages for the citizens of the County. However, if this type of reform is popular in other parts of the country then it may be imposed on Devon whether it wants it or not.

The County Council began as an organisation with a small staff and few responsibilities for direct service provision. Its main role was supervisory and it disposed of many of its duties through other public bodies. Virtually every change in the following ninety years expanded the direct service-providing role of the Council, though there were also some losses of functions, but in the last ten years the privatisation and 'opting out' movements have created forces which may cause a reversion towards the original system. As parts of services are 'contracted out', as 'direct labour' is redefined and as schools opt for a degree of operating autonomy so the County Council will come to work through bodies that are associated with it but are not integrated with the rest in the way that a section or office in a large department is.

Some analysts have written a scenario in which the success of the policy of handing over specific responsibilities to distinct bodies and groups – the local equivalent of 'hiving-off' and the 'quango' at national level – leads to a much more extensive programme of contracting out and leaves the local authority itself as the central co-ordinating agency for a large number of separate service-providing bodies, with only some functions, such as the coercive and protective services and long-term strategic planning, to administer directly. In this scenario the County Council will have a much smaller direct executive role and become a 'holding company' or 'indirect administrator', in fact reverting to the late nineteenth century system whereby county councils carried out many of their duties through other bodies.

Others believe that the experiments with contracting-out and hiving-off will prove a failure in some spheres and some areas and a reaction will set in in favour of direct administration by local authorities. They point out that the proponents of privatisation have forgotten the lessons of the nineteenth and early twentieth centuries. The role of county councils expanded almost continuously during the period from 1889 to 1960 because both the private sector and smaller local authorities exhibited many defects as service-providing bodies. The alternative scenario, therefore, sees the position of county councils being reinstated and reinforced after a period of experimentation with other methods of providing local services.

The County Council began in an era of complex party politics and within a local culture which was to some extent hostile to partisanship in county government. There is no doubt that party allegiances played a part in Devon's local politics in the first decade, and indeed the first twenty-five years, but it was a complex multi-faceted dimension of the local political system. Though partisanship was never entirely absent from the County Council it was restricted to a few divisions and sank almost to insignificance in the interwar period, revived slightly in the 1940s and then declined again in the 1950s.

Since 1973 local politics at county level in Devon has been party politics. It can be confidently predicted that this situation will remain as long as Devon exists in its present shape. But what of the party system itself and the balance between the different individual parties? Again a considerable degree of confidence is warranted in the prediction that, unless national politics is revolutionised, the system in Devon will oscillate between Conservative domination and a multi-party situation. The exact outcome of each quadrennial ordinary election will depend on when it occurs in relation to the cycle of Parliamentary elections with its associated variation in the standing of national parties in the opinion polls. The 1989 elections will be seen to have been crucial in determining whether the authority reverts to Conservative majority rule or continues as a multi-party system. If the latter then the members will have four years in which to evolve a set of longer-term conventions to regulate the roles of both 'government' and 'opposition'.

Devon started with a very small full-time staff whose heads were not openly prominent in county affairs. In the twentieth century chief officers have become 'public persons' in their own right and receive press attention as 'leaders' of the local authority, particularly in the spheres in which they are acknowledged experts or have a special responsibility. They are now supported by a large staff of professional, technical, administrative and clerical employees, and in some cases manual workers.

If the privatisation scenario is realised then the balance of work for heads of departments and their deputies will change. At present they fulfil many of their functions through subordinate officers organised in large hierarchies. If service provision is hived-off then their role will become less 'bureaucratic' and more 'political' – not in the sense of 'party' but as protectors of the interests of the local authority against associated agencies over which they have no direct control. The professional skills that will be particularly in demand in such a situation will be legal, statistical and financial, and the personal qualities those that make a good delegate or ambassador.

Early 1989 is not a good time at which to be writing about the future of the County Council as an organisation. The hundred years ends with pessimism and gloomy predictions for the future of county government, but these are nothing new for county councils or for Devon. I believe that the next four years are as crucial, in political and administrative terms, for Devon County Council as were the first two 'legislatures' of the traditional system.